CAN THE WHOLE WOMAN PLEASE STAND UP!

Overcoming Adversity Through Resilience and Wholeness

Cynthia Chirinda

Can the Whole Woman Please Stand Up:
Overcoming Adversity Through Resilience And Wholeness
Copyright © 2025 by Cynthia Chirinda
Reprinted Edition First published in 2017
This edition © [2025] Cynthia Chirinda

All rights reserved.

No part of this publication may be reproduced, stored in a retrieval system, or transmitted in any form or by any means—electronic, mechanical, photocopying, recording, or otherwise—without prior written permission from the publisher, except for brief quotations used in reviews or scholarly works.

Scripture quotations, unless otherwise noted, are taken from the Holy Bible, New International Version®, NIV®. Copyright © 1973, 1978, 1984, 2011 by Biblica, Inc.™ Used by permission. All rights reserved worldwide.

This is a revised edition of the original work.
Cover design done by Kudzai Kapenzi
Typesetting, and interior layout by Annie Nyamudzwadzuro.
Published in Harare, Zimbabwe.

For more information, author resources, coaching opportunities, or speaking engagements, visit: www.cynthiachirinda.com

ISBN: 978-0-7974-8017-9

CONTENTS

Dedication	v
Acknowledgements	vii
Introduction	1
Chapter 1 Standing Up Straight and Tall	3
Chapter 2: Beauty in the Place of Brokeness	7
Chapter 3: Embracing Your Authentic Identity	15
Chapter 4: The Profile of the Resilient Woman	23
Chapter 5: Celebrating Womanhood	31
Chapter 6: Creating Opportunities for Women— Divine Ndhlukula's Story	37
Chapter 7: Finding a Place to Belong—Beaulah's Story	47
Chapter 8: Escaping from the Jaws of Death—Michaela's Story	57
Chapter 9: Can You Find Self-Worth After Rejection?	63
Chapter 10: Who is Holding the Reins to Your Life?	69
Chapter 11: Who is Nourishing You As You Nourish Others?	73
Chapter 12: What Would You Do With a Second Chance?	83
Chapter 13: Can You Ride Above The Storms?	87
Chapter 14: Challenging the Status Quo	93
Chapter 15: Reflect and Rejuvenate	99
Chapter 16: What Type of Legacy Do You Want to Leave?	105

DEDICATION

To every woman who is determined to overcome adversity on her journey to pursuing wholeness.

ACKNOWLEDGEMENTS

There are many giants on whose great shoulders I continue to stand. From those strong shoulders I have experienced extraordinary mountain views and have also drawn strength to transverse through deep valleys. I would like to express my gratitude to every man and woman whose words of encouragement along my journey, have motivated me to write this book as I pursue my significant calling and life purpose. To the many women whose mentoring and testimonies have provided me with strength, guidance and inspiration, I salute the heroines in you!

INTRODUCTION

There comes a time in every woman's life when the whisper within becomes impossible to ignore. It is the whisper that questions the masks we wear, the roles we perform, and the boxes we've been placed in. It is the voice that asks: "Is this all there is to me?".

This book was born from such a whisper.

Can the Whole Woman Please Stand Up is a clarion call to women across generations, cultures, and backgrounds to reclaim the totality of their identity. Not just the polished pieces the world applauds, but the hidden scars, the unspoken dreams, the parts of ourselves we've buried under obligation, shame, and survival.

As women, we are often socialized to be fragmented—to compartmentalize our strength, our softness, our intellect, our faith, our desires. But true wholeness is found in integration—in standing tall in every part of who we are.

This book is not a roadmap to perfection. It is a journey into authenticity. It is an invitation to explore, heal, and embrace your God-given design. It is for the woman who is tired of hiding. The woman who is ready to rise. The woman who knows she was made for more.

Whether you are a student or a CEO, a mother or a mentor, a seeker or a survivor—this is your time. May every word in this book remind you that you are not alone, you are not too late, and you are certainly not too broken to be whole.

The world doesn't need another perfect woman. It needs a whole one. And that woman, dear sister, is you.

With love and purpose,
Cynthia Chirinda

Chapter One

Standing Up Straight and Tall

"And He was teaching in one of the synagogues on the Sabbath. And behold, there was a woman who had a spirit of infirmity eighteen years, and was bent over and could in no way raise herself up. But when Jesus saw her, He called her to Him and said to her, 'Woman, you are loosed from your infirmity.' And He laid His hands on her, and immediately she was made straight, and glorified God."

— Luke 13:10–13 (NKJV)

What Happened to Your Dreams?

Do you remember the version of yourself who used to dream without limits?

The girl who imagined the world as her playground? The one who thought anything was possible if she just grew taller, stronger, wiser, or more courageous?

Many of us begin life with hearts full of expectation. We were bold, imaginative, and alive with wonder. Then somewhere along the path, we began to shrink. Not outwardly, but inwardly. Life happened. Disappointments whispered doubt into our ears. Failure taught us fear. Society handed us invisible scripts that told us who we could and could not become.

The light began to dim.

Maybe the voices from your past still echo in your head, telling you you're not enough. Maybe life's demands have stretched you so thin that you've forgotten how to feel whole. Maybe, like the bent-over woman in Luke 13, you've learned to live with emotional and spiritual weight—believing this posture of heaviness is permanent.

But what if it isn't?

Does Anyone Really Care?

Have you ever sat through a worship service, surrounded by people, and yet felt completely alone?

You sing, you listen, you smile… but deep inside, you're asking: Does anyone see how much I'm hurting? Maybe your grief has become too familiar to those around you. Maybe their support faded as time passed, and now they assume you're "okay."

But you're not.

And you're wondering… Does anyone still care?

The bent-over woman in Luke 13 might have felt the same way. She had lived eighteen long years in a posture of pain. By then, people in the synagogue were likely used to her condition. But Jesus saw her. He called her. And He healed her.

That moment was her turning point.

And this chapter—this moment—could be yours.

Chapter Two

Beauty in the Place of Brokeness

Life can be a complex journey with many ups and downs. It is filled with both challenges and accomplishments. No one is successful at everything, just as no one fails at everything. We all have at least one thing we are or can be good at doing. However, when we go through challenging phases, we often dwell more on the bad experiences and end up feeling self-loathing and judgmental. Pitfalls are a part of life, whether we like it or not. What matters is that we don't bury ourselves in the grungy old pit and decide to spend the rest of our lives there. When life knocks you down, there are always two choices: Get up and move on or stay in that dark pit and live the rest of your life with resentment and regret. The latter will take you nowhere and things will probably get worse with time. Resilience is what makes the difference between those who survive and thrive, and those who don't.

Trümmerfrauen—The Rubble Women

Trümmerfrau (literally translated as ruins woman or rubble woman) is the German-language name for women who, in the aftermath of World War II, helped clear and reconstruct the bombed cities of Germany and Austria. Allied bombing attacks, which began in 1942 and continued until just days before Germany's surrender, reduced many German cities, like Dresden, Berlin, Hamburg or Cologne, to nothing more than tons of rubble. Although the war was over and the 12-year Nazi regime had come to an end, Germany was a country in ruins. *"You have to imagine that after the end of the war, the major cities were full of debri*s," said Bettina Bab, a historian specializing in post-war women's history. "95 percent of the houses were damaged or destroyed and there were huge piles of rubble on the streets."

Although it was normal that the survivors in the cities tried to make their homes liveable again and carted away debris in front of their door, this wasn't enough to clear the streets. "There weren't enough men to do this heavy work," Bab said. "At the end of the war, the German Reich was missing 15 million men." They had either fallen or become prisoners of war. So with the lack of manpower to clear the rubble, the Allied Control Council introduced a mandatory work duty for women, and they rose to the challenge.

Trümmerfrauen Faced A Gruelling Task

Long lines of women on the rubble piles, hammering out stones and handing them down in buckets was a common sight, even years after the war ended. But these so-called Trümmerfrauen, or rubble women, not only tended the wounded, buried the dead and salvaged belongings. They also began the gruelling task of rebuilding war-torn Germany by clearing the country's cities of an estimated 400 million cubic meters of debris, using only basic tools and, above all, their bare hands. "I remember that you could walk down Hohe Strasse practically on a mass of rocks that was as high as the first floor," said Käthe Lindlar, who was a Trümmerfrau in Cologne. "I was deployed in the Ehrenfeld district and had to load rubble with a shovel onto little wagons all day long. The debris was then put into trucks and driven away."

Are You Willing to Restore Order?

Who would have ever thought that women could take on such gruelling tasks in the rebuilding of a nation? Even in situations where the damage, disorder and chaos appear hopeless, women have been found in their communities taking up the toughest tasks to restore order. What does the rubble around you represent? What hopeless and seemingly insurmountable situations are you facing? Can you believe that you have been endowed with the grace and strength to stand up to the task so that you deal with the rubble that surrounds you? It may look overwhelming at first before you embark on the task of clearing the rubble. Your family, community and nation is waiting for you to strengthen your arms and clear the rubble as you pave way for transformation within and around you. How do you see yourself in your mind's eye? You are bigger and stronger than you think. The sight of it is traumatising. You need to arise as a mighty woman of valour to restore order!

The Trauma of Abuse

Located 146 km south of Harare on the main road south to Masvingo and South Africa, Chivhu (formerly Enkeldoorn) is a small town in Zimbabwe. Chivhu historically has an agricultural economy, based in poultry farming and dairy cattle. In this small town lies Mtoro, a ward sparsely populated by black medium scale farmers who purchased sizeable pieces of land prior to the Zimbabwe independence period. Owing to the rich pasture land, good farming soils and favourable climate, this area was a vibrant hive of activity which attracted diligent and hardworking farm labourers from different towns in Zimbabwe. In the Rhodesian era, the farm which my father bought as an investment was one of the most well renowned pieces of land boasting of a beautiful landscape with several streams on undulating slopes, an abattoir, a dam, thick vegetation a General dealer store with well-maintained infrastructure to support cattle ranching and farming activities.

Growing up as a young girl on the farm, rural life at the farm did not offer any special privileges especially for my unfortunate situation at that time. Routine tasks of farm work ensued daily under the direct supervision of my elders who were my primary care givers and the hired general hand who was from a foreign land. On the occasions that my younger relatives from Harare joined us at the farm at the end of the school term, it was always a welcome relief to have companionship and extra help with the tough rural life. Daily homestead routine tasks included rising early before dawn to release the flocks from their paddocks into the pastures and then resuming with water fetching duties before getting on with the seasonal farming tasks such as ploughing, weeding or harvesting grains from the vast acres of land. Age and gender at a farm do not attract any special privileges. If anything, the women folk tend to do more than their male counterparts. Such was the life that greeted me when I came into this world in the late Rhodesia era.

As the elders went about their daily routine farm tasks there was none to lend pity to this fragile young life that lived a life of solitude amongst the great company of bleating sheep, stubborn goats and strong willed oxen. The elders in my day had no time for frivolous complaints and anything that could have been easily perceived as laziness. The first time that I gathered the courage to tell one of my elders about the violent sexual abuses I was suffering regularly at the hands of the farm worker as I herded the flocks, she quickly dismissed me with threats of beatings and more. Knowing that there was no shield and rescue, these forced encounters continued unabated every time as we went about our daily tasks milking the cows, shepherding the flocks to different paddocks, drinking pans or pastures, fetching firewood in the forest or even at the homestead. No amount of screaming could alert anyone or bring rescue as the buildings and farms were far part from each other and there were thickets of tall grass and forests. At such a tender age I could never understand what pleasure a grown middle aged man could possibly derive from forcing himself on an innocent and tender young girl, too young to be in school and still continue this for years to come without any remorse or fear of being caught. He never did get caught or reprimanded and he continued to work at the farm for several years afterwards.

All I remembered over the years from the encounters were the putrid odours and helplessness that comes with any innocent creature being ravished by a heartless devouring rapist. The few times that I would be sent to spend the day assisting at the General Dealer store I would allow my mind to wander away to lands yonder as I would watch folks bustling to buy refreshments as they alighted from the Chigumba

AVM bus that faithfully serviced the Harare-Chivhu-Mtoro-Sadza route during that era. The hurried revving of the engine by the driver would make my heart race with excitement as though I was one of the passengers. I filled my mind with fantasies of life in Harare, escaping the emotional and psychological prison that had engulfed my world at such a tender age. With a loud threating horn the driver would rev more ferociously as the bus conductor made final rounds calling out to all the passengers in the store to return to the bus whilst securing on the top carrier loads of luggage for the new passengers boarding from the station at the store. The passengers would excitedly bustle back into the bus and I would look longingly at their cold, shapely bottles of Tarino soft drinks and fresh candy cakes topped with delicious pink icing on top. I contrasted this with the regular servings of "*Sadza nemunyevhe*" (Sadza with African spider flower leaves) which we would harvest freshly in abundance from the cattle kraal where it grew in abundance because of the fertile dung soils. This was alternated once in a while with the special delicacy of "*Sadza nehodzeko*" (Sadza with cultured milk) specially prepared by my grandmother. We only had mouthfuls of this delicacy when there were no visitors otherwise the children would have to scrounge around the "*mutuvi*" (cultured milk fermented extracts). As the bus drove away raising dust in the clean rural air, the sound of the engine would begin to fade away in the far distance and so would my excitement as I returned to the reality of the broken life I had. In the stillness of the night as my mind raced and as I tossed and turned in my bed I could still hear Chigumba droning in the distance. In my mind's eye I could see it spitting gusts of dust as it drove away from the Chirinda General Dealer store in Mtoro headed for Harare, the town of nights, renowned for her people who do not sleep. It felt as if the dust was laughing in my face and preparing to bury me in the dark misery of life in rural Chivhu.

From Brokenness to Confidence

Decades later having been blessed with a wonderful family, and by the saving grace of a loving God the trauma has dissipated. At the back of my mind I shudder to think how many young girls in different parts of the world face such brutality and violent ordeals with no one to protect them or shield them from such shattering experiences. The testimony of the power in the blood of Jesus which is able to heal all and restore full life has faithfully remained my beacon of strength and courage knowing that in spite of everything the enemy had designed for my destruction, God has taken every piece and beautifully fortified it with His unique craft to be used as a vessel to minister to other broken lives and exhort them to a place of confidence in the Lord. Even after having gone through this pain in my early childhood, the progression life brings with it countless curve balls. I have had to navigate through all of them standing on a solid and firm foundation of faith in order to overcome and come out strong. It is important to know that life is not about waiting for the storms to end, but learning to dance in the rain!

As you put your total trust in God through the pain, you will come out stronger and fortified with godly confidence. Confidence is not something that can be learned like a set of rules, it is a state of mind. Positive thinking, prophetic faith affirmations, practice, training, knowledge and talking to other people are all useful ways to help improve broken individuals to increase their confidence levels. More than anything it is important for individuals who have gone through painful violation to forgive themselves and accept that there is a new covenant of grace that brings restoration and glistening beauty in that place of brokenness in spite of the cause of their brokenness. Confidence comes from feelings of well-being, acceptance of your body and mind (self-esteem) and belief in what God has created you to be.

As we live through experiences which challenge and threaten to destroy us, how are we when we emerge? Some of us may have experienced in life some level of pain, abuse or degree of ill-treatment which shook us, broke us and possibly threatened our identity and wholeness. It is important to realise that we can cross over to yet another dimension of wholeness as we allow our spirit to grow in the knowledge of the Creator who created mankind in His own image.

MY RESILIENCE JOURNAL: PLANS AND STRATEGIES TO BUILD MY RESILIENCE

Chapter Three
Embracing Your Authentic Identity

Faulty foundations in self-definition and issues of authentic personal identity can cause individuals to feel like they are in a prison. The temptation towards self-hatred is highly destructive. Self-embrace does not imply that we overlook our areas of weakness and settle for mediocrity but rather that we forgive ourselves in areas where we have failed, accept where we are and apply ourselves to be the best we can be using excellence as a standard. When we fail to value, love and embrace ourselves it becomes very difficult for us to embrace love from others.

Working with individuals in their personal development pursuits I have recognised a common thread that haunts many individuals in spite of their race, age, tribe or allegiance and I have traced that to faulty foundations in self-definition and issues of authentic personal identity. One of the chief causes that can cause individuals to feel like they are in a prison emanates from prolonged periods of living fictional lives in order to measure up to unrealistic standards set by systems, culture, practices and people around them who enslave them to fit into unreasonable moulds. It is this same cancer that has destroyed innovation and creative thinking in families, organisations and communities.

The Fictional Life

Whilst many individuals may find it easier to fill the roles their family and friends expect of them, rather than becoming who they really want to be, living such a fictional life drains the critical life energy they need to pursue the things they truly value. The temptation towards self-hatred because of biological and physical attributes or other things that cannot be altered is highly destructive. I have met individuals who hate absolutely everything about who they are. They hate their body, their face, their hair, their shape, their voice, the way they move, their thoughts, and literally everything they do. They glow with admiration of everyone else around them but themselves. In some instances, others can even hurt themselves and a part of them feels great because they believe they are hurting something so horrible. Self-embrace does not imply that we overlook our areas of weakness and settle for mediocrity but rather that we forgive ourselves in areas where we have failed, accept where we are and apply ourselves to be the best we can be using excellence as a standard. When your behavioural life or your public persona is at odds with the vision, values, beliefs, desires and passions that define your authentic self then it is possible you may be living a fictional life that has you ignoring your true gifts and talents while performing assigned or inherited roles instead.

Dealing with Guilt, Shame, and Social Stigma

In chapter eight of one of my first published books, "*The Whole You—Vital Keys for Balanced Living,*" I write about the challenges of being disconnected by divorce. Fistfuls of statistics on divorce in our society and, unfortunately, in our churches do not offer solutions. Somehow, the divorced are expected to pick up the pieces, heal and get on with their lives. No matter that the dizzying prospects of providing and parenting leave little or no time to deal with tailspin emotions. It's no wonder many seek new relationships before they are ready. So what is the answer? I believe that the church holds the key to healing. After all, marriage was not designed by society, but by God. If the covenant relationship breaks, we need to go back to the Designer with the broken pieces. It's not the way it should be or how we want it to be. But, it's a fact of life. Hurting families are not statistics. They have faces.

> **If the covenant relationship breaks, we need to go back to the Designer with the broken pieces.**

There are circumstances which happen to people that are sometimes beyond their control in the relationships they're in. The definition of single mother is very broad—it can mean widowed, divorced or abandoned. The average woman will enter a marriage with a covenant mind set, with plans for "until death do us part." Divorce will not be an option for them. Yet, sometimes hearts harden. Sometimes people turn their backs on God's perfect plan for their lives. Sometimes one party makes choices that forever change a covenant relationship. Maybe there's adultery. Maybe there's abandonment. Maybe there's abuse. Always there is sin. You may have tried everything. You begged God, night and day, to save your marriage. You tried marriage counselling. You gave your all for years and years, and you never saw anything except continued adultery in return. You sought wise counsel from those who knew you best. You spent untold hours seeking wisdom from God before you finally walked away. I understand. I've lived through the hurt and the pain, the shame and guilt. I was once the "perfect" Christian. And then my life shattered. My family crumbled under the pain and shame of divorce. Your dignity is stripped away and if you are in ministry, that facet of your life drastically changes.

David and Lisa Frisbie, authors of "*Moving Forward After Divorce,*" describe how many divorced people, and especially those who hold strong religious values, tend to regard divorce as outward evidence of an inner character flaw. When we sin against a known law of God, guilt and shame serve the useful purpose of calling us to repentance and forgiveness. As we reflect on our own lives and conduct, God's Holy Spirit searches our hearts, showing us places and situations where we may have been selfish or sinful. As with all instances of revealed sin, we need to confess our wrongdoing and then move in positive directions, turning away from evil. In such cases, our sense of guilt is positive—it impels us to examine our hearts, renounce our evil ways, and repent—turning away from wrong choices and negative directions.

Yet often our feelings of shame are not rooted in a wilful act of rebellion against God or in a revealed sin. Instead, they may have their origin in the difficult circumstances of our lives, such as a divorce against our choosing. We may carry a vague sense of personal failure about being divorced; we may internalize a sense of shame or inadequacy that is inappropriate and unhelpful. Looking around at those who seem successful and capable, we may feel "less than" or "unworthy of" others. If we had somehow functioned better as a husband or wife, we reason to ourselves, we would still be married. Others can do this better, we may feel, but somehow we are incapable of succeeding at it.

In such cases, our sense of guilt or shame may entrap us—limiting our ability to function in normal and natural ways. By seeing ourselves as unqualified or unworthy, we tend to fulfil our own low and negative expectations. We may underperform, underachieve, and spiral downward into depression or other physical or emotional afflictions. In such cases, we need to break free from the sense of shame or guilt that imprisons us in the miseries of the past. We are likely to need outside help as we confront our misconceptions about our own identity and our own future. A trained counsellor or caring minister can be invaluable in the process of sorting through our feelings of shame. Without an objective listener, we may not make needed progress toward healing and recovery. Having access to an objective listener can mean the difference between stagnation and growth, between being stuck in the past and moving confidently toward the future.

Why Some Single Mothers Do Not Go To Church

In some western parts of the world, research and independent studies have shown that a large percentage of single parents do not actively attend church anywhere. Many single parents fear they will be judged. Whether unplanned pregnancy or divorce led them to become single parents (or some other reason), there is a fear that they will not be accepted by the congregation. Some single moms carry shame from past mistakes that may have resulted in their current situation. They fear they have somehow failed their children and forever scarred them. They cannot forgive themselves. Others feel that they do not belong.

The typical family that we all grew up watching on television consisted of a father, mother and happy children. Many churches are made up of similar families. Therefore, single parents do not feel there is a place for them. They struggle to find a place where they fit in. Unplanned pregnancy, oftentimes, is categorized as a more significant sin that perhaps lying, cheating, stealing, or any of the other sins that God detests. This, in turn, leads the church to believe any type of support for the single mother may in some way be promoting a "loose sexual lifestyle." We know that single parents can arrive at their journey in a variety of ways, just as diverse as the single parents themselves. Many have seen that Jesus did not come to save just the finely-dressed folks that are perceived as being sin-free, but rather came so that all may have life and have it abundantly.

Has Your Status Side-Tracked You From Your Purpose?

When we derive our identity from our marital status, health status or social status, we can easily lose focus of our authentic personal identity. When we allow our status to define us, we enter a seductive and dangerous space where we begin to seek for external definitions of our personhood. With these false definitions of our purpose also comes an incorrect understanding of what true happiness is. Leo Rosten said "I cannot believe that the purpose of life is to be happy. I think the purpose of life is to be useful, to be responsible, to be compassionate. It is, above all to matter, to count, to stand for something, to have made some difference that you lived at all." People seeking significance for their lives put an impossible burden on themselves when they try to build their identity from their own choices and intuitions alone. We just do not have the resources to give our lives purpose.

Purpose comes from God.

Knowing your purpose gives meaning to your life.

We were made to have meaning.

When life has meaning, you can bear almost anything; without it, nothing is bearable.

Without God, life has no purpose, and without purpose, life has no meaning. Without meaning, life has no significance or hope. Knowing your purpose prepares you for eternity. Many people spend their lives trying to create a lasting legacy on earth. They want to be remembered when they are gone. Yet, what ultimately matters most will not be what others say about your life but what God says. Can you confidently say you know your life purpose? Are you aware of your purpose and assignment on this earth?

My Resilience Journal: Plans and Strategies to build my Resilience

Chapter Four

The Profile of the Resilient Woman

What makes the difference between someone who barely survives tough challenges in life, and someone who meets these challenges head-on and thrives? It's the presence of resilience. The Merriam-Webster dictionary defines resilience as "an ability to recover from or adjust easily to misfortune or change," or "the ability to become strong, healthy or successful again after something bad happens." If we're going to get through the inevitable moments of difficulty in our lives, we need to learn how to recover and bounce back. Resilience gives us the ability to overcome obstacles and deal with difficult, life-changing events. It may require you to solve difficult problems, experience painful emotions or take action when you'd rather step back. But in order to overcome adversity, it is necessary to foster resilience.

How Can You Develop Resilience?

We all face difficult times at some point in our lives. Sometimes, adversity comes in waves, with one hardship or misfortune following another. These times can change our lives and challenge our beliefs about the world. How you act when faced with setbacks and hardships can be as unique as you are.

It may feel as if the obstacles you face are tougher to overcome than those of others. The reality is that every day, ordinary people are required to rise above their circumstances, dust themselves off and continue on. You can do it too. Worrying, anger, complaining, denial or any of the infinite other ways we try to circumvent pain when things go wrong won't change the situation.

Focus on building relationships. Studies have shown that strong, supportive relationships are one of the primary factors in resilience. Whether it's family, friends or co-workers, having role models, encouragement, support, love and trust is important to the ability to overcome adversity.

Accept change. When change happens, especially if it brings pain or hardship, it's natural to wish that it hadn't occurred. But once it's happened, continuing to fight the change only keeps you stuck in difficult emotions. Instead, try acknowledging that this change is hard, painful and unwanted. Then ask yourself how you want to live and what type of person you want to be going forward.

Try to learn about your strengths. Ask yourself how you've dealt with adversity in the past. Take time to reflect and build upon your strengths, then use them to your best advantage.

Act. Overcoming difficult circumstances can require us to take difficult action. Even if it's a very small step, it's important to move forward.

Avoid the victim mentality. Instead of asking, "Why is this happening to me?" we could ask if there's anything we did that might have brought on this trouble, or anything we failed to do, and we can make better choices, moving forward.

Stop blaming other people. When we blame other people for our difficulties, we give away the power to change things for the better. The more responsibility we take, the less helpless we feel and the more confidence we have in our ability to confront our challenges.

Do what's possible, when it's possible. Sometimes, the trouble we're facing is so awful that we can feel like giving up. Differentiate what you can and what you cannot change. Rather than focusing on the worst case, think instead of what else is possible.

Feel the burn. Exercise flushes out stress hormones, leaving us physically in a better position to face our problems. It also helps us emotionally, by flooding us with endorphins- the body's "feel-good chemicals," and by helping us to let go of pent-up feelings of frustration, anger or anxiety.

Cry it out. Crying is good for our physical and emotional well-being. It flushes out toxins through our tears, and helps us to face what's happening, accept our losses, and let go of our pain.

Take care of ourselves. Hardship is incredibly stressful, so we really need to focus on good self-care, like getting enough sleep, eating well, maybe getting a massage. And most importantly, we have to go easy on ourselves, especially if we notice that we're doing things a bit differently. This is a good opportunity to help someone else in need.

Create. Creativity is incredibly empowering, so it counters the helplessness we feel when bad things are happening. Pain is isolating, but being creative makes us feel more engaged in life.

Laugh. Humour is so good for our mind, body and spirit. It builds optimism and gives us perspective, momentarily bringing some light into the darkness.

Lean on your faith. Spirituality, meditation and prayer are calming, they can help us recover our strength and purpose when we feel lost, vulnerable or alone during difficult times.

Stick to the present. Rather than worrying about the future or dwelling on the past, focus on what is actually happening now and what is actually in your power to do now.

Valorie Burton, author of *Successful Women Think Differently*, describes five things which differentiate resilient women from the average women.

1. **Resilient women are authentic.**

    Resilient people are at peace with their humanity. Perhaps it's because their mistakes along the way have humbled them, or life experiences have helped them accept their own vulnerability, but resilient people don't let imperfections hinder them. They don't think failing means being a "failure." They learn as they go, making course corrections that lead them to positive outcomes.

    In what way(s) does God want to use your imperfections or challenges to exemplify His grace and mercy?

2. **Resilient women are flexible thinkers.**

    Even if occasionally, they struggle with negative thoughts, resilient women are self-aware enough to notice when their thinking is counterproductive. They don't fall into thinking traps such as jumping to conclusions or making assumptions. Instead, they gather the facts they need to move around obstacles and face the challenge head on. If something isn't working, they make adjustments until it works. They focus on the elements within their control and they exercise that control. So when faced with a cancer diagnosis, for example, they change their eating habits to aid in the recovery. When they get passed over for promotion, they find the grain of truth in the boss' negative review and start making improvements.

In what way is God calling you to be more flexible?

3. Resilient women are (mostly) optimistic.

It is hard to bounce back from setbacks when you see every obstacle as the end of the world! Research shows that optimists live as much as nine years longer than pessimists. Seeing the bright side's good for your health and longevity. But it isn't about simplistic "positive thinking." The essence of optimism is at the root of faith, "the substance of things hoped for, the evidence of things not seen" (Hebrews 11:1). We must believe something good is possible, even as we prepare ourselves to withstand a storm. Proverbs 22:3 says, "A prudent man sees danger and takes refuge, but the simple keep going and suffer for it." Resilient women see risks and take precautions to prevent problems. But when faced with a challenge, resilient women are more likely to say, "I can get through this," whether it's a tough class at school, a relationship challenge, or the loss of a loved one. The average woman does the opposite—she allows setbacks and disappointments to discourage her to the point that she stops hoping for something better. And when you stop hoping, you start settling.

> **A prudent man sees danger and takes refuge, but the simple keep going and suffer for it.**

In what way(s) have you stopped hoping for something more or better? What is it time to muster the faith and boldness to hope for again?

4. Resilient women reach out.

Resilient women don't go it alone. They have close friends and aren't too proud to ask for help when they need it, talk out problems, or help others in need. When faced with a stressful situation, just knowing you have support can alleviate the pressure. Iron sharpens iron. Strengthen your relationships. They make you stronger.

In what way(s) are you going it alone? Who do you sense God wants you to reach out to?

5. Resilient women use their strengths.

Everyone has innate talents and strengths. When faced with a challenge, there's power in tapping into those strengths—the God-given gifts that come naturally to you. It takes less energy to use your strengths, in fact, you are energized by your strengths. Know what yours are and use them.

What strengths has God blessed you with and how could you use them more effectively in the opportunities and challenges you face?

My Resilience Journal: Plans and Strategies to Build my Resilience

CHAPTER FIVE

CELEBRATING WOMANHOOD

A ll around the world, International Women's Day represents an opportunity to celebrate the achievements of women while calling for greater equality. Each year International Women's Day (IWD) is celebrated on March 8. The first International Women's Day was held in 1911. Thousands of events occur to mark the economic, political and social achievements of women. Organisations, governments, charities, educational institutions, women's groups, corporations and the media celebrate the day. So, what exactly are we celebrating on March 8th again? Are we celebrating progress? Are we celebrating the roles of a woman? Are we celebrating the various functions? There are varied forms of abuse and oppression that a woman still tolerates. Oppression is more than not saying NO. It could also mean excessively saying YES, as is the fate of many women who wear multiple hats in today's world. While today's woman is juggling between various roles, she is still struggling to find her footing.

The Epidemic of Overwhelm

Today, most women are juggling several jobs: breadwinner, family caregiver, family health manager, cook, and more. Whilst some men are beginning to contribute more to household chores and childrearing these days, many working women still feel they have to be superwoman and are burdened by an epidemic of overwhelm. So are women more resilient than men? Do we have some inner resource we can call on that helps us sustain? Or do men and women get equally overwhelmed by the pressures of life today? Building a reservoir of resilience gives you the confidence to know you can make it through a potentially stressful situation; it gives you the energy to continue down the road after stress drains you; and it gives you the ability to quickly reset your system to perform in a normal, operational state.

> **Building a reservoir of resilience gives you the confidence to know you can make it through a potentially stressful situation.**

Unmanaged stress is a prime disabler of resilience. Your resilience depletes when you feel resistant or compressed. Your resilience also depletes when you let your emotions spin out of control or add more drama to stressful situations than is helpful.

In these changing and uncertain times, inconveniences, impatience and frustration can stack into overwhelm and drain your emotional resilience. This can lead to health problems that further sap resilience. To survive as superwoman or thrive as a balanced human being, we need to build up our resilience capacity.

Grooming Women for Leadership

Whilst Grooming is generally defined as the process of making yourself look neat, attractive and presentable, there is more to it than meets the eye. True grooming which is sustainable and enduring is not only external but rather a transformational process that starts from within the inner person. Leadership is about knowledge, skills, and abilities for transformation. It is also increasingly about worldviews or visions of life—beliefs, values, and principles. Shockingly, in this era, there still exist individuals and institutions who question whether women have what it takes to lead. Society needs to understand that women were not created as an afterthought, but were deliberately created on purpose to exercise the dominion mandate given to mankind by their Creator. Women were born with the innate ability to not only reproduce but to incubate, nourish and amplify ideas. Deliberate efforts should therefore be made to develop the leadership capacities of women from a young age to enable them to engage in positive nation building. As we celebrate women, we want to see women who are envisioned and empowered so they can play a significant role in the socioeconomic development of their communities and nation. Women who are equipped to understand their purpose and the vital role they can play in the development of their communities and their peoples. We need to see women meaningfully collaborating with men in their communities to enable transformative leadership and holistic socioeconomic development.

Do You Know Your Purpose?

In his book, "*Understanding the Purpose and Power of Woman,*" the late Dr. Myles Munroe states that "When purpose is not known, abuse is inevitable." Being a woman who has had to juggle various roles as wife, mother, career woman, pastor, amongst many other, I understand the pressure that women face as they set out to balance their different roles and pursue significant lives. The answer is found in understanding your purpose, vision, values and priorities. In the pursuit of success, you can set up yourself to be abused or become your own enemy when you do not understand why you were placed on this earth. When you understand your life purpose, vision, and mission whilst remaining consistent in your values, your walk will testify the glory of God in every service you provide and product that you produce.

The Unique Fabric that Unites the Family

Women are the fabric that holds families together. The family is the fundamental unit of society. It is the foundation upon which the state is built. The cultivation and promotion of family ethics and values such as love, care, loyalty, generosity, obedience, sincerity amongst others in individual families will gradually transcend and transform the whole nation. Family ethics and values must be cultivated to preserve the important institution of the family. The family is an important structure in the development and moulding of society. It is in the family that one learns how to exercise authority and submit to authority and from the family these virtues are translated to the state. This is why we need women to be whole so that they can competently play this critical role. In life, anything that you want to achieve is going to take time and, most importantly, effort. Time is our most valuable asset and if we are truly invested in something, our efforts and time will be all we have to offer. Nothing comes easy in this world and if we really want something, then we are going to stop at nothing to make it happen. Finding your passion may be the most difficult part of your life, but once you find it, you will stop at nothing to make your dreams come true.

I challenge my fellow womenfolk across the globe to arise in the knowledge of their authentic personal identity and to take on their positions for the sake of our sons and daughters who are looking and learning from us. We must change our conversation and become relevant to the present and future of our nations. We must move away from the petty level of conversations we have been known to engage and start prioritising high seat issues which add value to the national discourse. We must indeed become impassioned with technology and extraordinary things beyond our comfort zones.

MY RESILIENCE JOURNAL: PLANS AND STRATEGIES TO BUILD MY RESILIENCE

CHAPTER SIX

CREATING OPPORTUNITIES FOR WOMEN — DIVINE NDHLUKULA'S STORY

"If you want a certain future, go out and create it. Conquer your fears because fear is what enslaves most women. As women, we need to roll up our sleeves, lift our feet, and carry ourselves."

Divine Ndhlukula

Securico Women's Day 2017 was a day of celebrating how far the organisation had come in a sector previously considered not suitable for women. It was an afternoon of fun and lots of inspiration. What a moving testimony from Mwanabenge, one of SECURICO's Super Women who lived to the billing of the theme "Being Bold for Change," as she gave a presentation on her real life story of struggle and triumph! She narrated how she had travelled the road to death in 2007 just before she joined SECURICO having had the knowledge of her HIV status. She was kicked out by the husband after having tested HIV positive. She had started giving away whatever she owned in preparation of her "impending" death. As she walked the dusty roads of Mabvuku, she saw an advert for security guards' recruitment and what made her respond was one of the benefits stated as "Good HIV/AIDS awareness and support policy"

She struggled to finish the rigorous training with the help of the instructor who understood her condition. On this women's day in 2017, Mwanabenge celebrated numerous achievements over her years of service since she joined the organisation. Amongst any other achievements, she is the anchor of Securico's peer educators. She has built a 3 roomed house in her rural home and now owns 6 head of cattle. She has named three of them Securico, SHEQ and Quality. Mwanabenge is happy she works in an environment where colleagues remind her to take her tablets when its time. To add icing on the cake, she shared with everyone how in 2015, she met her significant life partner who went on to pay lobola (bride price) to her parents a year ago in 2016. In her own words "ndakaroorwa kunge mhandara" (I was married like a young, fresh bride). She boldly stated she has never been happier in her life.

As the owner of a security firm that employs approximately 4000 workers, with a large portion comprising of women, and with multiple business merit awards under her claim, it is befitting to say that Divine Ndhlukula (nee Simbi) is a top dog in a male dominated, dog-eat-dog business environment. Purposeful and gritty, Divine is a rarity amongst women of her generation. Even her parents knew they had produced a gem, the moment she was born in her rural home in Gutu. Her father exuberantly told everyone who cared to listen that "this girl is going to be something in life; she is going to take care of the family."

"I always wanted to excel in whatever I did. I knew that I wanted to do something that was not just ordinary and I was very ambitious," she confided with The People of Zimbabwe Handbook. So when others were dreaming of becoming housewives, nurses, teachers and mothers, she wished to be a manager and to run her own business, and God answered her call. "I was a born leader from a young age. I'm a natural leader. When we were going to school or playing, I was the one to dictate the pace. I would lead people and decide when it was time to work or play. "I would just naturally and effortlessly lead others within my group. I enjoyed it because it made me feel in charge. "I would always be telling people that I am going to run my own business. I would say that I would work for a maximum of two years and then start my own business," she recounted.

During her wedding, she remembers that whilst it was considered tradition for new brides to cry, she did not shed a tear but simply smiled her way to the altar. Divine's entrepreneurial spirit was awakened early on. At her various working stations, she bought clothes from factories for sale to colleagues and friends. Realising there was a gap in the security industry, she started Securico in 1998 from small savings, initially with four employees from the cottage of her home. From humble beginnings, Divine has over the years steered Securico into arguably the most ubiquitous security company, providing cutting-edge electronic security and guarding services. The company has scaled dizzy heights—becoming the first security company to be ISO certified, in addition to bringing a professional feel to the industry that had never been witnessed before.

In starting her own business, Divine was inspired by the few successful women during her childhood. "My role model was my primary school teacher Ms Madzima who seemed independent and another woman who was a magistrate Mrs Machingura. I would look up to these women and feel inspired." This also included her own mother Mbuya Mary Simbi and her auntie the late Fadzai Simbi. A holder of two MBA degrees, her journey to the top was not without bumps along the way, and Divine overcame gender discrimination and several other challenges. "I did not have a salary for the first 6 years of the business. I sold a house to ensure that this business went ahead, and at some point when my husband died, I moved to my sister's house and stayed with her for a year. I had to live on a shoe-string budget to make sure my business was up and running.

"The other major challenge was prejudice but one should have the ability to deal with people who look down upon you. If you are not strong you can easily back track. Fortunately, I am not that kind of a person. I am not one who gets affected by that kind of behaviour." Widowed in 2001, Divine says determination and encouragement from her husband spurred her to succeed. "My husband died in 2001 and if it were not of him, I would not have started Securico. "At the time I was conceiving the SECURICO idea, my husband was diagnosed of kidney failure. I had to give him support, was working fulltime and planning to start this company in a sector I had no prior experience in. I then decided to abandon the idea of the security company as it was just too much for me then. However, my husband gave me strength, saying I couldn't stop living my dream on his account. He told to me to go ahead and start the security company. While she was still in mourning, eight days after her husband's death, her only operations manager then, Sabion Ndou, was murdered. She had to quickly pick up the pieces and rush back to work. "I worked much longer that I had planned, and continued to work until I made a breakthrough. It was not easy. I had to work 8 hours at work and 8 hours to do my business and still had my 6 hours to sleep."

The Securico founder grew up a women activist in rural Gutu where she was fortunate to continue with school. "The policy to employ women was conceived right at the beginning. I had always been an activist even when I was growing up. I grew up in the rural areas, I was fortunate that my father could afford to take all of us to school." She laments how she would see a lot of the girls she grew up with having to drop out of school between Grade three to Grade Seven. Some of the girls would be married off and Divine was grieved by the injustice in all this. During the first days, she literally begged clients to accept women as their security personnel because her desire was to empower women, who at that time were not easily accepted in the industry. Today Divine has set a record of being one of the highest employers of women in Zimbabwe and she is delighted to see them empowered. "Some of them come from very bad backgrounds, widowed and left to cater for the children and some even with the HIV virus. But I feel satisfied that I have managed to give hope to those who had lost hope and are empowered to take care of their kids and families, that's my greatest satisfaction when I look at them." Divine believes that one of their greatest achievements as an organisation is the acceptance of women in the hitherto male dominated sector. With almost seventy percent of their board comprising of women, thirty-eight percent in in middle management and fifty-four in line supervision, the organisation consistently demonstrates the visionary's firm belief in women empowerment. "Some husbands support their women but others still would like to divert women they feel what we are doing or the field they have chosen has too much power such that the feminine aspect disappear."

She says her parents were instrumental in moulding her towards success. "My mother taught us to work hard. She made sure that we would wake up early in the morning to do all the household chores. She told us that hard work did not kill anyone so we would shine the floors until we could see our faces." "My father on the other hand was one of my greatest motivators. As I attended rural schools in Gutu he motivated me with money each time I came first in class. He would give me two and six (25cents)—a lot of money then, which inculcated the sense of working hard and getting rewarded then. When I went to secondary school he made sure I attended the best schools as I was a very bright girl"

The self-actualised businesswoman says she wants to be remembered for the positive effect she has made to other people, in particular, women. "I have worked with women who have never dreamt that they would be somewhere. I recruited women who were timid and had to instil in them the mind-set that they can make it. I had to hold them by the neck and say to them you can do it. When we started some of the girls would not have wanted to be seen by clients. "When I was growing up I was aware that many girls and women in society were getting a raw deal in terms of opportunities. So when I came to Harare after college, I was conscious of the lack of opportunity for women. "I could see so much injustice and I told myself one day I could change it."

In addition to empowering women she works with, Divine is very involved with the women economic empowerment agenda through various organisations where she mentors and inspires women to dream big and help them scale up their businesses. A member of the Methodist Church in Zimbabwe, Divine is a very family centred person who seriously takes the role of bringing together her family that includes her mother, her siblings and their spouses, their children and their spouses and other extended family members now and again. A natural leader who effortlessly lead others, Divine regards as her role models those women who have done great things ahead of her. "Such women have opened the path for us because you can only aspire to be somewhere when you have seen others who have made it and look up to them and say that's what every other girl or woman should aspire to be. Hope Sadza is one of my greatest role models and on the entrepreneurship side, my role model is Kubi Indi."

For all the years she has been in business, Divine says she has learnt that nothing comes easy. "While I knew I was going to make it in business, I had not really anticipated the amount of hard work, discipline, commitment and determination I needed to get where I am. I have had to learn that the secret of success is found in one's daily schedule. "I believe that every good deed is a door opener hence I always try to be as good as I can to others. My key to success is loving and connecting with people which are always the seeds of great things to come. I believe in playing by the rules all the time and most importantly upholding my personal integrity as this gives me a good night's sleep."

She is a very much sought after speaker as an entrepreneurial expert globally and she enjoys sharing her story with all and sundry as a way of influencing more women and young people to go into starting up their own enterprises. For those who aspire to triumph in business she says: "Work your plan with passion, determination and diligence, and when a bit of cash starts rolling in, have the discipline to know that it is not your money yet."

Ndhlukula does not even call her core employees guards because, she contends, their work is much bigger and more complex than just guarding. "We don't call them guards. They are called operatives because they operate different things. When you get into a bank, you're expected to operate as a banker. We go into the mines and we're expected to operate as miners and be able to understand the key issues in mines. If you leave an operative at your premise, he's the one who is going to ensure that if there is a burst water pipe, he's going to be a plumber. If there is going to be a fire, he is going to be a fireman," she boasts. Despite having climbed up the ladder of success right to its pinnacle, defying the dictates of a male-dominated society, she has not forgotten the thousands of women scraping a living right at the bottom of the ladder. Divine is a true champion of women's empowerment in Zimbabwe and is currently the largest employer of women in the country outside the government sector, with over 900 women employees on her payroll. She pioneered the Women's desk at the Zimbabwe Chamber of Commerce where she is a deputy President. This was after the realisation that woman did not network at the level of the major Business member organisations like ZNCC, CZI etc. This is the platform she has founded initiatives live the WECA (Women in Enterprise Conference and Awards) the Mentorship in Practice, and Woman Owned Brand that links women enterprises to sustainable markets.

My Resilience Journal: Plans and Strategies to build my Resilience

Chapter Seven

Finding a Place to Belong — Beaulah's Story

My childhood was really tough. I was taken to my grandmother in the village when I was only six months old. My grandmother had to nurse (breastfeed) me. I stayed with my grandmother and rarely saw my mother. At one point I was raped by a neighbour and never told anyone. Sometimes I would be moved from my grandmother to either of her brothers that had farms in the surrounding area.

My uncle, who was my aunt's husband, came to take me to live with them in town, when I was seven years old. I stayed with them for the whole of my Junior School education. I would go to my uncle's village with his children every holiday. They had their own share of problems, at one time my aunt uttered something that I will not forget. She lamented that she was still in the marriage because she had to look after me. At this point I was only in grade five, and as a young child I started having these thoughts of how I had become a real burden to people. I rarely saw my own mother and wondered how these people under whose care I had been place thought of me.

After Junior School I proceeded to High School, where I was placed in boarding school. During the school holidays I would still go to my uncle's village to stay with them. He was such a good man, he treated me like his own child. It was only after I had completed my High school that for the first time I started to stay with my mother. It was at this point that she was now trying to be a mother, and in her view, being a mother purely translated to exercising strict discipline. Being a teenager who had grown with so much pain and anger bottled inside, we were always at crossroads and I would not take anything from her. The relationship was very strained. I remember her saying to me during one of her "dress me down" lectures, that I had been obstacle to her getting married as no man wanted someone with a child. At this point I felt that this was a confirmation of why she had dumped me and left me with my grandmother.

I went on to pursue my tertiary education as I was staying with my mother, but we had no close relationship at all. When I started working my mother declared that my salary was hers and therefore she is the one who kept my bank "passbook" as we called it that time. She justified this by saying it was because she sent me to school and thus wanted to get her money back and enjoy the benefit of sending me to school.

So I would still be given transport money like a child and she would still go and buy me clothes using her credit account. I tried to speak to my uncles, her brothers, but it just did not work because she would challenge them, asking which one of them had ever contributed even a safety pin from my infancy. It was because of this attitude that their hands were tied and they just minded their own business.

I then met a man, who later became my husband. Due to my situation at home, I wanted to get out as soon as I could. He really appeared to be a gentleman having been born in a neighbouring country and seemingly different from some of the local men I had seen. Coming from a "well to do" background with parents representing the country and being posted to different nations. He would boast of the exploits of his family and the life they used to live. He had however, not finished his education and had used the influence of his father to get a job in one of the biggest firms in our city. He did not have a good job since he was not qualified at all but, I really saw potential in him as we spoke and he would agree to go back to school.

Since I was so desperate to leave home and was getting a better salary, I took the initiative of getting us a rented apartment, then moved in together with him. I went on ahead to furnish the apartment and was virtually doing everything. He used to drink, but I thought he would stop once we started living together but instead, it became even worse. I got pregnant with twins and it was a blessing that my job had me covered for almost everything, medicals, doctors, and hospital. The day that I gave birth he went and dropped me off at the hospital, in labour, and went for hours and only saw him hours after I had given birth. All this time I kept on hoping things would change. He would become physically abusive, and would hit me for any slight thing. You would say a statement or a joke and it would turn to something else. I remember one time he found me in the bath, I cannot even remember what he asked me but I remember seeing blood coming out of mouth and I lost one of my bottom teeth. I remember telling lies at work the following day that I had been involved in a car accident and lost my tooth.

I look back and see that he had a problem with the fact that I was getting a better remuneration than him. He was aware of his weaknesses, but instead of addressing them he would attempt to demonstrate and show that he was a man by exerting physical force. I would defend him to my relatives, and ended up cutting communication with most of them because of that.

The children grew up and I had to still run around to look for places for school, their fees, our rentals and domestic upkeep. In all this there was no appreciation at all from him, instead he would criticise everything I did and say that he would have done better. I started engaging in small business entrepreneurial activities in addition to my formal work. Whenever I would present an idea, he would water it down through his negativity. I would discard the ideas sometimes, but in the end I realised that if I did not rise up and strengthen myself to pursue my vision, my children will never go to school let alone have a decent life. Because of the background he was brought up in, each time he would get money he would want to prove to people that he too could make it and he would buy expensive things and lend to "friends" who would not pay back. Sometimes this was at the expense of the children's fees or our upkeep. He was too generous to a fault to prove himself.

Years later in our marriage and serving in leadership roles at our local church, I had thought that the responsibilities and spiritual pursuits would bring about transformation in his outlook on life. Sadly, each time when I would ask what plan or vision he had for himself or his family, he could never be in a position to articulate it. All he would say was that he could only plan when he has money. So from him never came a plan or vision as the head of the home. There was not sustainable stability in his activities. He started going outside the country pursuing 'deals' that never brought anything. I would borrow money to send him whilst he was out of the country. At one time he went for four months, the people he had gone with returned but he stayed and I had to borrow money against our car to send to him again.

We sold one of the houses which my mother had left me after she passed on, in order for us to start a business. Being someone who did not have any business acumen and had refused to go to any school to develop business management skills, we ended up losing the house, the business collapsed and we started reeling in serious debt. We sold the remaining house but still nothing significant materialised through lack of planning and the know-how of how to run the business. We were homeless, our property was attached, and we started living with his friends. All this I would try to hide it from my relatives to protect him. The last straw came when everything was now shutting down on us, he just left again like going on one of his so-called 'deals' and went for four years. During that time he would not even ask how we were managing, where we were staying, or how the children were coping. He would not even bother to make an effort to contact our different landlords as the man to negotiate for his family or apologise for non-payment of rentals and bills. There were so many creditors pursuing me since he was gone.

In the end I realised he was an unreliable runner who would run each time there was pressure or problems. It really hurt because as a wife you would expect the man in your life to fend for you and protect you and family. He chose to leave and abandon us just exposed like that.

I looked after his mother who was terminally ill, and since we could not afford a private nurse and she would mess herself. I had to do all the cleaning up and bath her, but still he would not appreciate all that. Instead he would compare me with other women or his friends' wives.

To these women he was a hero because he could run and do errands for them or drive them wherever they would. On the other hand, I had to walk, commute and use public transport to do my business as I could not use the car because it did not have any fuel or he had to use it for something. So in the eyes of everyone else he was such a generous and helpful man yet he failed his own family. When he abandoned us, not even once did his friends ask how we were coping or thought of buying even a mere loaf of bread.

Empowering Other Women Through Tough Experiences

This season of life was extremely distressing. Had I not continued to hold on firmly to my faith in God, I could have easily lost my mind. In spite of my pain I continued to minister the word of God and strengthen other women to arise and become economically empowered. With the few resources that I had, the knowledge and experience gained through my entrepreneurial endeavours, I had the opportunity to impart life skills to women who felt they were in hopeless situations. Women coming from impoverished communities were able to come together and start meaningful internal saving and lending schemes. Some of them started running home bakeries, others upgraded their informal meat selling businesses and formalised their butchery business plans through the practical training programmes we established in the communities. It was extremely fulfilling to see women who never thought they could have a meaningful economic livelihood begin to open bank accounts and take care of their children. Some of them started investing in assets and their mindsets completely shifted from a place of hopelessness. A door of opportunity opened for me to leave the country and start a new life. As I look back I realise how much my life had been broken in several places yet I had not given up and continued to pick up the pieces and move on. Decades later, I am grateful for the opportunity to start a new life and find my whole self again. I realise now that there are some times when you have to move away to find yourself again. Even though this was a difficult decision to make because of my attachment to my home country, I realise that just like the ten lepers in the Bible, if I had stayed in my situation I would have ended up in a ditch or a beggar somewhere.

Shunned Like a Disease

The shunning from those I had done much for, especially in the church, the shame, the belittlement and neglect brought a deep wound in my life. During the peak of the dark season in my life when everything around me had crumbled and my husband had just abandoned me and the children, there were few friends to be found. Even the friends I thought were in my corner started becoming uncomfortable when they were seen talking to me. Because of the situation of lack that I was now in, the people I previously had in my circles became very distant. Those who were married started keeping me at arm's length as if by merely coming near their husband I would snatch them away from them. I did everything I could to maintain my grooming and presentation in spirit of the weight loss from the stressful situations. It was only by the grace of God that I continued to fellowship with my church mates because I refused to have my spiritual identity stolen from me through the struggles in spite of the rejection I experienced. I kept on in spite of the reproach, shunning, shame, humiliation and pain and emptiness. I would worship and just open my heart to the Lord. Some people from church actually came up to ask why I was still attending the same church after all that neglect and reproach. Deep inside me I knew that God was dealing with some issues at the core of my being. I later heard some people commenting on how they admired me for my strength and resilience. They did not know that I was just a walking shell feeling very empty inside but I was determined to find wholeness.

I Am a Living Miracle

One day I received the sad news that a certain lady I knew to be healthy and strong had just passed out and died at the veranda of her house. This got me thinking that despite all I had been through I was still alive and still very sane. I began to realise that there was a real reason for me being alive. And that there is a real purpose I am on this earth. I know we all say we were born for a purpose or call. But just wait till you go through the storms of life. You forget all that. I began to see how my resilience was impacting other people's lives and encouraging them. I began to see my eyes opening to opportunities I had have never taken, had it not been because of what I went through. My eyes began to open with a complete different vision. Had I still been in those relationships which represented a comfort zone perhaps I would not have 'dared' to take the leaps of faith I did or make the significant sacrificial decisions I then took towards finding wholeness. I began to really understand what those lepers in 2 Kings 7:3 went through. Sometimes it really takes desperate situations to take desperate measures. I began to realise that it is not what I am going through or what I have been through that matters but how I can use this same situation to leave a legacy for my children and those looking up to me. What a joy it is to be able to spare someone's life and have it reawakened because of your own experiences.

Finding Wholeness In a New Lease of Life

An opportunity opened up for me to really make a drastic and sacrificial decision. Usually with major decisions like that one would have to seek counsel and affirmation from other people but from what I had been through and the fact that no one would think anything good would ever come out for me. I had to turn to my own sister, who had seen and gone with me through these hardships. Her being a fighter and having also gone through a real rough patch became my pillar as I began to push my way through this door to open and after a real struggle, the door opened for me, somewhere I had never dreamt of in a nation I never in my wildest dreams thought I'd ever live. Getting here was a real struggle and I am still pushing to attain that which I was called for here. Helpers have come up to assist. A new page has opened up and I would not be here had I not risen up to take stock of my life and to take the drastic decision I took. Had I looked for an audience to confirm that it was the right decision for me to do would I have been where I am today? Some would have said with nothing to my name I could never accomplish such a significant move. Others who had written me off would have wished me to still stay in that same situation. Others would have feared for me, and the "spiritual ones" would have said that is not God's plan. Yet deep down inside I know that I made the right decision towards my life calling and towards the next dimension of what I placed on this earth to be and become.

My Resilience Journal: Plans and Strategies to build my Resilience

Chapter Eight

Escaping from the Jaws of Death— Michaela's Story

"To anyone out there in an abusive relationship always remember that your safety and well-being is more important than your status."

My story begins with a teen pregnancy at 16 dropping out of Lower six form, due to the pregnancy and going off to get married. I gave birth a week before my 17th birthday. I turned 17 as a mother to a beautiful girl but with no life skills to generate any income and only relying on my husband's salary. The First year of marriage was fair, then the abuse started. I would get beaten for simple things like not asking why he came home late and when I would ask, I would get beaten for asking.

I enrolled for school through Rapid Results College wanting to further my education and that was met with a lot of resistance. One day I got home to find my books being used to start a fire and that was the end of my pursuit. The abuse went on for two years. The day I walked out of the marriage my husband had not been home for over 3 days and he had not communicated anything. I left home on a Saturday morning and went shopping with my daughter. I got home to find that he had returned home about some minutes after I had left the house in the morning. He began to hurl insults and then started beating me using the lid of a wooden laundry basket which broke into pieces each time it landed on my body. He then stabbed me on the right thigh with a knife in full view of our daughter and it was at that point that I decided that enough was enough. He then left the house and I went to speak to his brother. My brother-in-law had heard the noise and altercation but did not intervene. He instead advised me to stay on and that if my husband should beat me again, then I should seek intervention from the family aunts. I decided that I was not going to wait for another opportunity to be beaten so I took our daughter and left for my parents' house. I was welcomed back home and a representative was sent from our family to his to inform them that "mwana wedu tatora (we have taken our child), don't bother coming to apologise or to persuade her to return." On the following Tuesday I had to go and write exams. I went to into the exam room with a body that was battered and a swollen blue-black face. In spite of what had transpired I managed to pass my exams.

The Transition

The transition was not easy because I was coming from a situation of relying on a husband to provide and now I was back at my parents' house economically disempowered. I decided that I was not going to put an additional burden on them so I started working in a hair salon whilst pursuing studies for a secretarial course. I managed to pay for my daughter's preschool. The abuse did not stop just because I had left his house. He would try to assault me if he saw me, and I ended up going to seek a peace order after he had tried to run me over with his car. I was informed that since our marriage was a traditional marriage the only way to formally break the union was through giving him a divorce token, (gupuro). My family facilitated for that to be done, so I went and gave him the divorce token.

Taking on New Roles and Responsibilities

I worked in the salon for two years then I decided to pursue a job in formal employment. I worked as a secretary for five years then I made a career move and was started working as a Personal Assistant. Life dealt me a major blow when I lost my parents to HIV/AIDS. My father passed on in 2006 and my mother in 2007. I was left with sole responsibility of raising my four siblings and my daughter. Tatenda was in his 2nd year at the University of Zimbabwe then. Gamu was in her first year at the same institution, whilst Nigel was sitting for his Ordinary level exams when my mother passed away. The youngest, Evans was in Grade five. My daughter Ashley was in Grade four, when my mother passed away.

I had to be strong for everyone else. It was not easy but God sustained me through that season. I got to know God in all facets and experienced Him in His various names, as Jehovah Jireh, Elohim, Jehovah Shammah, and El Gibor.

God of the Second Chance

Truly God is a God of the second chance. In 2013 whilst I was minding own business serving in the house of the Lord. My "Boaz" saw me and we started courtship, got engaged and I subsequently got married to the King of my Castle, Jeff. He treats me like the queen that I am. He encourages me to pursue my dreams and to grow deeper in my relationship with God. In 2014 I took up voluntary retrenchment and I started operating a catering company on a full time basis. The business has its ups and downs but the last few years have been a learning curve for me. At the time of publishing this book, my siblings had made great strides in their careers and lives. Tatenda got a scholarship to undertake PhD studies in Biotechnology, he is currently single. Gamu completed her Economics degree and is now a married mother of one, she is working in Harare. Nigel is due to complete his Economics degree this year (2017). Evans is in Qatar taking a gap year before he proceeds to Belgium to do his Accounting degree having attained fifteen points at A level. At the time of publishing this story, Ashley my daughter is due to start her Culinary Arts studies at an institution in Cape Town. Sixteen years ago, if anyone had asked me where I would be in ten to fifteen years' time, I would not have known what to say. All I can say is that God has kept and sustained me. My steps have been ordered by the Lord.

To anyone out there in an abusive relationship always remember that your safety and well-being is more important than your status of being called "Mrs." In all trials that you may face God is the only answer. He is the one who can line up divine connections and divine appointments as you put your trust in Him.

MY RESILIENCE JOURNAL: PLANS AND STRATEGIES TO BUILD MY RESILIENCE

Chapter Nine

Can You Find Self-Worth After Rejection?

In life as we pursue the deep sense of belonging, we can easily become engulfed by the overpowering desire to be found in the company of others as we shun our own company. Social connections are beautiful, warm and often comforting. When we are in the pleasurable company of our family, friends, acquaintances and colleagues, we become engaged in other matters and dialogues that often take us away from the present realities in our own lives. Social connections are necessary for our vitality. Nevertheless, our personal development is threatened when our over-indulgence in social company takes over the precious moments that we ought to invest in times of reflection, reviewing and planning ahead. Apart from the need for social connections is the desire to belong to a team, an organisation or an institution as a vibrant member. Sometimes we are denied this opportunity when our applications to join, subscribe or find employment are rejected, suspended or discontinued for one reason or another.

The Pain of Rejection

Rejection wounds hurt deeply because rejection attacks the very person that we are. It destroys our self-esteem, our self-value, self-worth and our purpose in life. Rejection has a way of destroying a person's life in a way that few other things can. The sad fact is that the number of people who are affected by rejection is staggering. If we want to be all that God has created us to be, then overcoming rejection and its effects is vital and absolutely essential. Whether you have experienced rejection from the womb, from childhood, in a dating relationship or marriage, the wound of rejection creates a doorway for unwholesome activities in your life which need to be addressed and closed for you to find wholeness. The wounds of rejection can open a person up to many other destructive forces. Rejection can result in performance orientation, rebellion, violence, self-harm, sexual promiscuity, sexual perversion and other extreme behaviours. Lack of love as a child, for example, can cause that child to turn to pornography and lust to fulfill their need to be loved.

The Dynamics of Rejection

The closer a person is to you, the deeper their rejection can wound you. Authority figures are also able to deeply wound you, because you look up to them and rely upon them. Whether you love or hate a person doesn't make anybody immune from rejection. You can literally want to kill somebody, but still be affected by their rejection. The question is, are you looking to them for approval? Are you basing your identity upon what they think of you? Does their approval of you give your life meaning and purpose?

A person's age also has a lot to do with their vulnerability to rejection. Children are especially vulnerable to the damage of rejection, because they are still developing their identity and learning about who they are. A lot of damage is done by peers in school. Insecure children can be very cruel and damage other children through rejection. Why? Because their own identity is not based on the right things. They do not know who they really are, or who they are called to be, so they go around putting other kids down to make themselves feel better.

Dealing with Rejection

You cannot settle rejection issues fully until you get it down into your spirit that you are accepted, loved, and appreciated by God. Tearing down the strongholds of rejection is as simple as merely receiving, with childlike faith, what God's Word has to say about your identity, who you are as a new creature in Christ, who is called to life, purpose, and meaning in Christ. The one thing that you absolutely cannot overlook is correcting your identity. You need to start seeing yourself for who you are in Christ, and the person that God has really formed within you. Your identity must come from Him and what His Word says about you. Forgiving those who have rejected you is a starting point, even when they have not approached you to ask for forgiveness and even when they fail to acknowledge the pain they have caused you.

Dealing with Curve Balls

A curve ball is an unexpected interruption in the normal routine of life. Life's curve ball's come from a variety of sources. We need to expect the curve balls and the interruptions in our lives with the understanding that changes WILL happen. Even if you're a creature of habit that thrives on routine, there will be times when routine goes out the window and reality takes on a whole new shape. Some changes will be challenging. Very challenging. These times can be trying, but they can also be rewarding. You might discover a hidden talent you didn't know you had. Or you might just impress yourself with how much you're really able to handle when it's thrown at you. These are all awesome self-discoveries waiting to happen! When a change is looked at as a fresh opportunity and a chance to learn something new, it's no longer quite as scary. Even if you had no intention of ever pursuing this new direction, embracing rather than resisting is always the method of least resistance. You should always keep an open mind because what initially sounds like a complete disaster might end up being the best thing that ever happened to you. Without an open mind you could miss the opportunity. Maintaining a sense of humour during difficult times also helps put ourselves and others at ease, and that right there is half the battle won. In times of stress and struggle your own personal care might be the last thing on your priority list, but it shouldn't be. Taking time out to treat yourself to something that makes you feel great really does help the healing process.

While you may feel like curling up in a ball and staying inside forever, getting out there because embracing your new reality will actually feel a lot better. Your life is an adventure worth pursuing, so don't let setbacks, even major ones, derail you completely. Take the time to acknowledge and embrace the change and then get back to take on life again. In every situation you are in, there are always factors that you can control and factors that you can't control. What are the factors that you can control? Focus on them. What are the factors that you can't control, but which you can influence through their contributing factors? Focus on them too.

> **If life has dealt you a curve ball, do not wait until the dawn of a New Year for you to find yourself again.**

If life has dealt you a curve ball, do not wait until the dawn of a New Year for you to find yourself again. Invest in some contemplative moments and do some soul searching as you review your year and plan ahead for the coming season. Are you able to identify the things that drain you and leave you with a feeling of emptiness inside? Are you doing anything to address those energy and emotional drainers? Have you ever suffered from rejection in your life? Do you feel that you have dealt with it from the root? How much alone time do you give yourself in a day or a week? What voices are you listening to and which frequencies are you tuned into? What could be distracting you from listening to the vital voices in your life? How wholesome is your self-talk?

My Resilience Journal: Plans and Strategies to build my Resilience

_____

_____

_____

Chapter Ten

Who is Holding the Reins to Your Life?

Since we were born, our minds have been gradually programmed by our surroundings and by society at large. As we grow, evolve and awaken to this reality, we learn that it is in our best interests to uninstall some of this programming and take back control of our minds. We need to take control back from the immense amount of cultural, societal and institutional brainwashing that has greatly influenced who we are and how we view ourselves and our abilities.

Failure to regain control over our lives can directly lead to a sabotage of our future.

Are You Calling The Shots in Your Life?

During one of my 2016 year-end goal setting workshops, I had brief conversations with some of the participants and asked them what their plans for the festive season were. When I sat down later to assess their responses, I realised that whilst most of them were still indecisive about how and where to spend the festive holiday, almost all of them had relegated the decision to other third parties and external forces outside of themselves. Whilst they had the full prerogative to make this simple decision as grown adults with the capacity to lead their lives and families, they had still made the decision to leave it to other individuals and external circumstances. Sadly, the outcomes of such indecisiveness often leads to an unfulfilled life where it is becomes second nature to blame others for one's expected failed outcomes. When you give over the responsibility for significant life decisions to third parties and external forces it is highly likely that your life will follow a trajectory that you did not expect, want or desire from the onset. To whom and to what external forces have you handed over your life to make major life decisions for you about when to move, shift, stay or maintain the status quo?

Conditions versus Decisions

Whilst some of the circumstances we find ourselves in are not entirely of our own making, the sum total of our lives is usually a reflection of the decisions we have made. Each time we make a powerful decision, we step more fully into our own unique, authentic expression. We have the power to change our lives with our decisions. Some would argue that our conditions are the larger part of determining our destiny.

Whilst our conditions may be relevant, it is important to note that for any situation one person claims shaped their destiny for the worse, there are counter-examples of people who used their decisions and action to overcome those same circumstances. If you think your life and its conditions is holding you back, whatever seems to be preventing you from reaching your full potential is more likely your decisions (or lack thereof) than your circumstances. There are blind folks who are climbing mountains. Double lower leg amputees dancing, walking and running. Conditions can be overcome, with decisions, creativity, determination, and hard work.

Every Decision Shapes Your Future

Every decision and every choice shapes your future, from what you eat, to where you work and live and especially the people you spend your time with. Everything in your life, business and personal, exists because you first made a choice about it. Despite our parents making most of our decisions for our better and brighter future when we are very young, we start learning early how to choose between the options placed strategically in front of us and make decisions. The present is a gift you need to make the best of, and the core of your future comprises each and every decision you have ever taken. Sometimes we don't allow our mind to think and we make choices too fast. Other times we just want to follow the crowd or to be a popular in the way we make our decisions. We should allow our minds to think through our decisions. Decisions affect and shape our character because our decisions become our habits and that becomes our character.

You Are Responsible for Your Life

Powerful decisions are not easy, but making them grants us access to what we most long for—to feel empowered, authentic, and capable of stepping beyond what we believe ourselves to be. What powerful decisions have you made? What did you learn in the process? How have these decisions changed your life? It is our decisions, not the conditions of our lives that determine our destiny. You are the Chief Executive Officer (CEO) of your life. You are 100% responsible for your life; its happiness; its wealth and health. You choose the Executive Officers, also known as the people who will support and help you the best way they can throughout your life. Evaluate the people in your life; then decide which relationships to promote, demote or terminate. In the absence of constant examination of what we carry as cargo in our individual lives and corporate entities we run the risk of using up much needed resources on dead wood at the expense of our strategic vision, goals and plans.

My Resilience Journal: Plans and Strategies to build my Resilience

CHAPTER ELEVEN

Who is Nourishing You As You Nourish Others?

Imagine what your world would be like if you felt deeply nourished in your body, mind and soul. You would undoubtedly be vibrant, radiant, powerful, confident, sensual, energetic, unstoppable and impactful in every area of your life! God has uniquely created women with an innate ability to not only reproduce but nourish life. As women we are often pulled in every direction, stretched well beyond our limits, and expected to keep our emotions—and everyone else's— under control. And that's not always so easy to do. But if you can learn to disconnect from the stress of everyday life to invest a few moments in yourself, then you'll find that you are better able to handle all the curve balls that life throws at you.

Nourishing pertains to supplying with what is necessary for life, health, and growth. Women are powerful agents for nourishing as they cherish, keep alive, strengthen and promote others. Sometimes we pour ourselves so deeply into the lives of the people we love around us. We devote so much time to ensure that our children, siblings, husbands, family members, friends and church members are well taken care of. When we look around we may find that there are so many people who are fully dependent on us for their well-being and we have become a primary source of their nourishment. It is praiseworthy for us to be aware of the needs of those around us and for us to respond by carrying each other's burdens as we are commended by the word of God in Galatians 6:2. We should not neglect our duty of nourishing others, however, it becomes unwholesome when we do these acts of service at the expense of our own vitality and well-being.

When Paul sent an exhortation to Gaius in 3 John 2, his desire was to see his fellow labourer in the gospel living a well-nourished life on every level and in every area of life. As women with full lives, tons of responsibilities, and a natural tendency to take care of everyone else—sometimes we don't take care of ourselves the way we deserve. Very often we find ourselves reaching for the food that's simply available instead of the food that's truly nourishing. We also have a tendency of staying up getting that one more thing done, instead of getting to sleep to replenish our bodies. Some of us wish we could shed some unwanted weight yet feel enslaved by our cravings. In our self-talk we are not always very kind to ourselves - we throw insults at ourselves instead of loving ourselves. As a result, we tend to find that the people around us begin to treat us with the lack of kindness that we internally reflect within ourselves.

Nourishment During Life's Transitions

The transitions of life are inevitable. How we navigate them can further the emotional turmoil or transform us into a better version of ourselves. The book of Ecclesiastes in chapter 3 does teach us about the different seasons of life. When we are going through emotional crisis, one of the best things we can do is to nourish ourselves - body, mind, and spirit. This will provide us with the fuel we need to sustain us and carry us through to the other side. This is the time to be mindful of what we are eating, and fuel our bodies with foods that will serve us. Depending on what you may be going through, sometimes you may experience a complete loss of appetite, this is understandable. This is a good time to explore the right supplements to ensure you are getting all of the right vitamins and minerals your body needs. Just remember your body needs love too, and fuelling it right will help you look and feel your best as you weather the storm. Most of us know what, how and when we should be eating for maximal health, but the key to long term transformation is shifting our mindset and creating a new identity that matches our physical transformation. Yes, we want to look and feel our best, but if we don't work on our mindset, any health program will be thwarted and we will inevitably end up sabotaging our efforts. Nourishing your soul is just as important. We all need to find time to quiet the mind and embrace activities that drown out the noise so that we can hear that still voice inside. How are you feeding your soul and what are you doing to nourish your spirit man as you go through life's transitions? How committed are you to your daily spiritual disciplines? Are you committing enough time to pray, worship and develop your intimate relationship with God? How much time are you devoting to studying the word of God and allowing its power to cleanse, heal, encourage, sharpen and direct you? Have you maintained your fellowship with the body of Christ so that you can nourish your spiritual gifts and receive edification from others? Have you surrounded yourself with Godly associations that can minister to you?

Are You Willing to Expel What Contaminated You?

In life, the things that contaminate us the most are not necessarily agents that force themselves on us. Growing up in rural Zimbabwe herding goats, sheep and cattle—one of my greatest life lessons in those years spent with nature in solitude is that the things that damage us the most are those worthless deposits that we fail to expel from our system until they become toxic enough to destroy us at the core. Whether you have ingested abuse, betrayal or unfair treatment from an individual or organisation you need to make a choice to release it from your system before you become toxic. Release it all and allow the freshness of your Creator's promises to restore you to wholeness.

From my experiences in herding flocks one of the most important things I learnt is that you always have to be alert of the animals' whereabouts and what pastures they are feeding from at any given time. Failure to do that could result in very grievous episodes. I used to herd a very stubborn bunch of goats that would not hesitate to stray to the nearest vegetable garden that caught their sight if you just allowed yourself to snooze for a moment. Some of these gardens would have been sprayed with poisonous insecticides. I also used to have a very notorious but exotic Brahman bull that had a knack for eating plastics. It would spend days thereafter in constipated pain until it got human assistance to expel the plastics from its system.

Sometimes we find ourselves holding on to negative things in our lives for longer than we should. The negativity we entertain in our lives will impact us as a whole person and causes us to be burdened with a sense of this dread and negativity in our everyday lives. We need to understand that whatever does not nourish our soul should not find place in our lives any longer. Whilst it is hard to let go of things we are attached to because of the fear of dealing with consequences of letting go, we risk contaminating and damaging the image of God that should be made manifest through us. Take time to examine your life and identify the things, people, places, events and circumstances which no longer nourish your soul and to start the process of lovingly releasing these things in your life. Remember whatever you let go of will always be replaced by something good or better.

Are You Still Processing Toxic Files?

There are some damaged files that we keep processing in our life's central processing unit which we should have trashed out of the system days, weeks, months or decades ago. Yet sadly we continue to allow them to circulate in our system, regularly passing through our most delicate, vital and precious organs to be pumped out back again into the veins of our thoughts, feelings and emotions. Who would we really be blaming for the toxic waste we carry in our hearts and thought life? These toxic substances are responsible for the lack of wholeness we experience in our bodies and emotions which is why some of us have many hidden toes and venomous tongues and emotions that erupt at the slightest provocation. When we

> **When we continue to replay files of trauma we can only expect to hallucinate even in our most wide awake moments.**

continue to replay files of trauma we can only expect to hallucinate even in our most wide awake moments. Naturally this intoxicated condition repels the good and well-meaning people in our lives. Even more, this paradigm will attract those things that we claim to detest and abhor the most because our state of toxicity emits certain fragrances in the intangible realm which attract the very disorder that we claim we don't want to have in our lives.

Detoxing Every Life Dimension

The act of erasing requires a determined effort to completely delete what you do not want to see manifesting. We cannot expect anyone to undertake that action for us because we ourselves are better acquainted with the writings that exist on the walls of our inner being. Detoxing all these life dimensions requires a boldness to confront issues and a deliberate personal effort to remove what you don't want to see in your life. The root of our contamination lies in the damaging things that we internalise and allow to take permanent residence inside of us. Once they take permanent residence in our internal realm they derail and corrupt our progress. Whilst we are not computerised devices that encounter programme errors and hang, admittedly our life processes periodically inject certain viral objects into our system. As we advance into each year in our lives, our progress or lack of it will be determined by the efforts we make to not only confront the things that have contaminated our wholeness but to delete, erase and reset our life controls for a refreshed and wholesome life.

You Are Responsible for Your Nourishment

When you nourish something, you supply it with what is necessary to sustain life and growth. What fills your soul with life? Which hobbies, activities, or daily rituals bring you joy or a deep sense of satisfaction? If you take care of yourself, if you get support, if you nourish yourself… the people in your life will benefit. Those people will then positively impact others and we can be assured to have nourished families, societies and nations. When you are well nourished you will think better, feel better and make better decisions. Live a truly nourished life and feel vibrant and alive!

Pillars of Wellness

More than ever before, we hear about wellness in the media, in conversations, and even the workplace. When we think of Wellness, we think of well-being, wholeness, and balanced health. We think of a self-awareness that causes us to be at peace with ourselves and the world around us, with a focus on holistic health. What is Wellness? Wellness is an active process of living a fully engaged life at every level of being. It is becoming aware of, and making healthy choices toward a healthier state of life. Life is not one component, but many parts working together. Abe Brown, founder of Momentum Coaching, shares the concept of seven pillars of Wellness in the WHOLifE Journal.

1. Relational Wellness—How You Connect

How we connect with others is critical to our own sense of health and well-being. We each need between 8-10 meaningful touches per day to be mentally and emotionally healthy. No wonder so many people feel like they're missing something! Relational Wellness speaks to healthy conflict resolution, social intelligence, effective communication skills, and the capacity to be truly intimate.

2. Mental Wellness—What You Think

We are what we think, and become the product of the thoughts we consistently embrace. Happy people work down to the detail of their daily thought life, and teach themselves how to think healthy thoughts consistently which empower and inspire them. We need a health Mental & Emotional Support System; a system of thoughts and beliefs which support us in our dreams and aspirations.

3. Emotional Wellness—How You Feel

Emotions are not thermostats but thermometers. They are not root causes, but are symptomatic of underlying issues. However, the way we feel has a huge impact on our level of motivation, our actions, our behaviours, and our results. Take time for emotional management, emotional intelligence, relaxation, and healthy thinking, which leads to healthy emotions.

4. Physical Wellness—Physical Health

Our body is our temple. We are responsible to take care of it, and treat it with respect and tenderness. If we do this, we will generally have healthy outcomes which will enable us to lead a fruitful life. Physical wellness leads us to focus on healthy nutrition, regular sleep, regular exercise, and self-care.

5. Spiritual Wellness—Values & How You Treat Others

The best measure of your spirituality is not the church, mosque, or temple you frequent. The best measure is how you treat others. It is walking with integrity, honesty, fairness and compassion. Respect. Kindness. Authenticity. Gratitude. Selflessness. It is also taking time for personal reflection, meditation and prayer.

6. Professional Wellness—What You Do

Professional Wellness is far more than the money you make or the title you hold. It is a sense of living in alignment with your "LIFEFIT": your unique combination of gifts, abilities, passion, education, and life experience that makes you who you are. It is being fully yourself, and making money as you do!

7. Financial Wellness—What You Have

Financial Wellness is not a certain number of zeros in your bank account or driving a certain car. It is abundance. True abundance is having enough for you and those you love, and being able to contribute to the needs of others. We need to make a resolve to weed out unhealthy habits of excessive debt and poor money management choices, and promote healthy choices of stewardship, saving and investment, building assets, and planning for the future.

8. Community Wellness—What You Contribute

Martin Luther King, Jr. said that, "Life's most persistent and urgent question is, 'What are you doing for others?'" As humanity, we are not designed to be like the Dead Sea, with an inflow but no outflow. We are designed to contribute, add value, and render service to the world around us. The truth is that we all have a unique contribution, and we are happiest when we are making our greatest contribution. Though each one of us will contribute something different, our rewards in life are generally in direct proportion to our contribution. So, another quote from Martin Luther King, Jr. will help us in terms of what and how we contribute: "If a man is called to be a street sweeper, he should sweep streets even as Michelangelo painted, or Beethoven composed music, or Shakespeare wrote poetry. He should sweep streets so well that all the hosts of heaven and earth will pause to say, here lived a great street sweeper who did his job well."

Wellness is a process in which you build these 8 Pillars into your life. Wellness is the way that you approach each day, and what you do proactively to stay healthy holistically. Don't live in a one-dimensional fashion because you are not a one-dimensional person!

MY RESILIENCE JOURNAL: PLANS AND STRATEGIES TO BUILD MY RESILIENCE

Chapter Twelve

What Would You Do with a Second Chance?

If you had a second chance - the opportunity to do something over and do it differently - what would you choose to do over and what changes would you make? In life, the opportunity to erase the mistakes of the past and start over are a rare occurrence. Typically, your actions result in consequences, whether they are good or bad. Everyone makes mistakes. But not everyone is given an opportunity to make things right. Not everyone gets a second chance. That is why if you are given the opportunity to fix your wrongs, you should be careful and play your cards right. Remember that you can never make the same mistake twice because the second one was a choice. This is true. We have to learn from our mistakes so they never happen again. If an opportunity comes for you to do something all over again, can you do away with the things that you did wrong?

What Do You Regret?

A hospice nurse compiled hundreds of hospice patient responses, highlighting the top five regrets people had who were dying. "I wish I'd had the courage to live a life true to myself, not the life others expected of me." "I wish I hadn't worked so hard." "I wish I'd had the courage to express my feelings." "I wish I had stayed in touch with my friends." "I wish that I had let myself be happier." Easier said than done, right? We don't think twice when we complain to our co-workers about another 60-hour work wek, or when we have the best intentions to call that valuable person we haven't seen in a while and lost touch with. But the truth is, life doesn't come with a do-over. It doesn't come with an endless string of opportunities or a giant eraser that cleans the page. So when the time comes, whether you are 35 and diagnosed with incurable brain cancer, or a hundred and two, celebrating your birthday with three generations of family and friends, and someone asks you, "Would you do it all different"—would you? And after you ask yourself this question, will it be too late?

How Have We Managed Our Relationships?

None of us are perfect. As human beings, we make mistakes; some of a trivial nature, some a lot more significant. But we make them. And sometimes these mistakes affect other people and we have to ask for their forgiveness. But what happens if someone else makes a mistake that affects us, and we have to decide whether to give them a second chance? At many times in our lives, we will upset others; we will anger them, hurt them, bother them, disappoint them, or let them down. But then there are other times where we make them feel appreciated, cared for, and we give them all we can. We only try to live the best life we can, we try to make others happy the best way we know how; but sometimes we get it wrong. As do the people around us. However, when someone shows remorse, shows genuine promise that they are willing to try to change; that is when they might deserve a second chance with you. It is up to you whether you want to take that risk. The important thing for you to realise is that they could hurt you again; you might even regret giving them a second chance. BUT ask yourself this, what would you regret more—staying, but risk getting hurt again? Or walking away and losing something that may have been worth keeping?

Make It Right

If you get a second chance, do everything you can to make things right this time. Avoid the things that led you to the mistakes you've made and go the right path this time. Make sacrifices just to prove you deserve the chance you are given. Remember that every opportunity has a shelf life. If you waste a second chance at fixing a wrong then you may never be trusted again with another chance.

Making the Best Out of a New Season

In this season of your life, have you reflected on the things that you could have done differently during the year and are you willing to change in the New Year? Are you able to make those changes by ourselves or do you require new skills together with support and guidance? Who and what do you need to change about your interactive network and social circles? Have you already set goals for the current year and beyond using integrated thinking to plan for every area of your life?

MY RESILIENCE JOURNAL: PLANS AND STRATEGIES TO BUILD MY RESILIENCE

Chapter Thirteen

Can You Ride Above The Storms?

We live in a time when everyone has a message, a revelation, an opinion, a theory, and a point. When you log onto your social media, turn on the radio or television, you will experience a flood of different voices with a plethora of different messages, all of them trying to convince you to receive their words. Why? Because they realize that you are indeed going to listen to someone, and whomever you listen to will have great influence and control in your life.

We also live in a world where opportunities present themselves on a daily basis. They continuously float around us. Very often, we choose to watch opportunities pass us by each day. And most of the time, the only thing holding us back are the voices we have chosen to listen to.

Embrace the Eagle Mindset

When the storms come in, the winds increase, the Eagles will ride above that storm and use the strength of the wind to fly higher and higher. You could be facing some storms today and not sure which way to turn. When you embrace the eagle mindset you will know which voice to listen to. Eagles are not intimidated by storms, they know they can use those storms to take them higher. If you have that mindset, as you face your storm, that storm will turn from something that threatens to break you into something that will transform and make you. A chicken, on the other hand, does not have the ability to fly. It is usually cooped up in a chicken coop and fairly happy in its little world. When the storms come the chicken will go running; anything to get away from difficulty. Chickens are small minded, small hearted and have limited vision. Eagles on the other hand can see far the distance. They have a vantage point that a chicken will never have. It can be very easy to get to get bogged down with the difficulties and busyness of life. Be encouraged to take a step back and reflect on the voices that have shaped your mindset. What do you need to change so that you can start to see things differently?

Who Are You Flocking With?

The Law of Attraction or the Law of Magnetism would say that you attract and surround yourself with people similar to yourself. Have you ever stopped to wonder if the people you have surrounded yourself with is indicative of the type of person you are, or whether you are a product of the group of people around you? Did you draw them to you, or did you change to become like them? What have the people around you helped you to become? Have they lifted you or brought you down. Do you feel happier around them or more negative? Do they have the same types of goals that you do? Are they positive and uplifting? Do your friends make you want to be a better person? If the people you associate with don't push you to be better, then it is highly unlikely that you will have the energy and support to follow your goals or dreams. But when you are surrounded by people who are motivated to improve their lives, you will suddenly find that you are more productive and proactive about chasing self-improvement. Just being around them makes you want to work harder towards your goals so that you can feel comfortable in the group.

Chickens Walk, Eagles Soar

You have many choices in life and one really important one is choosing to be an eagle or a chicken. Eagles soar with other eagles high above the clouds and are fierce, while chickens scratch on the ground and walk around with other chickens not doing much of anything. Thomas Carlyle said that "the block of granite which was an obstacle in the pathway of the weak becomes a stepping-stone in the pathway of the strong." This saying definitely describes the difference precisely between eagles and chickens. Eagles look at the obstacles in life as just stepping stones towards their own success in helping others and accomplishing their future goals. Chickens give up easily and tend to be fragile and don't stay the course when difficulties present themselves. Eagles adapt to forever changing environments and rise above adversity with others like themselves. They fight for what is right and do not allow the opinions of others to get them off their journey and obtaining their desired goals. They take life by the horns and do not worry about getting cut because they know their own value and worth. They are strong willed, brave, confident and create opportunities for themselves when previously there were only walls. Eagles ask others for help and remain humble enough to celebrate their own success without boasting. Eagles ask others how they succeeded and what steps to take to obtain the same results differently. They invest in themselves by spending money for their brands, companies and personal development. They don't take no for an answer and deal with rejection as being one step closer to a yes. They create solutions for people problems and then we take massive action to implement their brilliant ideas, putting them to use for the greater good.

Are You Plucking Away At Life?

While chickens seem to have fun just plucking away at life and walking around aimlessly with other chickens, they don't get very far in life because they give up too easily. People that are like chickens are scared to try anything new or take risks. Chickens get distracted too easily and ultimately end up doing what is easiest. Chickens continuously make a lot of noise but hardly ever accomplish anything. Chickens don't have a lot of self-esteem and allow other chickens to get them away from their journey because they quit before they even finish any task or significant goal. Chickens don't positively condition their minds to compartmentalize their priorities, schedules and projects to maximize good use of their time. Chickens allow the opinions of others to define who they should become. Chickens learn to rough it and become accustomed to staying and living mediocre.

There is a clear depiction of polar opposite characteristic traits amongst eagles and chickens. It is much more difficult being an eagle because nothing worth having comes easily but it will be worth it. If you are hanging around people that are not on your level, you will not receive the proper nourishment for your spirit, mind or soul and will eventually die of malnutrition. As you make daily decisions about which voice to listen to, remember that the chicken coop is too restrictive. You are designed to be limitless and not to be limited. If you are not living out your God given purpose, you are limiting your growth and expansion. Are you going to fly like an eagle or will you remain in the chicken coop? The choice is yours.

MY RESILIENCE JOURNAL: PLANS AND STRATEGIES TO BUILD MY RESILIENCE

Chapter Fourteen

Challenging the Status Quo

People love to be in their comfort zones. Once we find a particular way of doing things, we are very reluctant to change the way we go about it. If you review biographies of some of the world's most successful people, you will find a number of character traits that they all have in common. Generally, these individuals have a vision—they know what they want to accomplish or what they want out of life. They set goals and they work hard to achieve them. They think positive and learn from mistakes or failures rather than using them as excuses to give up. These individuals remain focused on their objective and look for ways to overcome barriers or solve problems that would otherwise keep them from achieving what they set out to do. They are not terribly concerned about what others think of them or their ideas. Above all, they don't quit. Self-determination is a combination of skills, knowledge, and beliefs that enable a person to engage in goal-directed, self-regulated, autonomous behaviour. An understanding of one's strengths and limitations together with a belief in oneself as capable and effective are essential to self-determination. People who lead significantly successful lives use creative strategies to reach their goals. They look at options and make informed decisions. Successful planning requires that you know your responsibilities, strengths and challenges; set goals; work toward those goals; and use tools and resources available to you. What are you willing to do in order to get out of your comfort zone?

Challenging the Status Quo Is a Mind-Set Shift

When you challenge the status quo, it means that you identify new and better ways of doing things. It also means that you add value, and that's the very basis for being successful. Challenging the status quo is a mind-set shift which you can bring about by being conscious about how things operate today—and by proposing a new and better way of doing things. One of the best ways of bringing about this mind-set shift is to regularly take a step back and ask a set of insightful questions. Set time aside in your diary and allow yourself to get away from your desk for 30 to 60 minutes. Go to a place where you feel inspired and where you will not be disturbed. Take a "balcony" view and observe it from afar. What is working well and what is not working so well? How could you run it in a more successful and effective manner?

Learn to Ask Good Questions

Asking the right questions can lead to eye-opening insights that are right there waiting to be found but that no one has taken the time to find out. Avoid asking yes or no questions, always giving people an opportunity to give you lots of detail. Follow up initial questions asking people for their opinion or insight. Progress from Why to How, Where, What if, and more. Don't just scratch the surface with your questioning. Go deeper until you get to the real heart of the matter. You will also need to be willing to shift your perspective. If we never change our perspective, we will never grow.

The Potential of Unlimited Success

When you consistently challenge the status quo, you have the potential of unlimited success, because you add an unlimited amount of value. You also have the potential to demonstrate your leadership skills, because you make things happen based on your vision. Thought leaders are not satisfied with following others or doing a "good" job. They are committed to excellence and they see things better than they are. They make their own models of how things should be and are brave enough to implement these models.

Don'T Just Think Better…Think Differently

Keep in mind that even if you don't see an opportunity for massive disruption in your existing or desired space, you can still create a competitive advantage through minor disruption. How can you become more disruptive and challenge the status quo in your industry? Begin with asking why. Asking why repeatedly will lead you to a reason for an action. If the "why" is weak, you are onto something. Searching outside of your industry or even outside of your country offers insight into how others are thinking differently about the same challenges.

Be Bold and Brave!

Going after any firmly held beliefs does not come without pushback. Your willingness to speak out against these principles immediately sets you apart and provides the opportunity to present other new ideas you are bringing to the field. Being disruptive can be scary. It is not for everyone. Every single leader, movement, and organization that has ever wanted to create greatness has had to challenge the status quo. Challenging the status quo takes an open mind, open heart, and open will. To make a difference, to have an impact, and to become great we must do the unorthodox thing. To move from mediocrity to greatness, we must venture out. To build something substantial, we must take a strong stand. To create something meaningful, we must create significance. Nothing great is ever achieved by doing things the way they have always been done. To challenge the status quo, we must take one fearless choice at a time, one brave decision at a time, one courageous action at a time. These choices, decisions, and actions transform challenges into exploration, risk into reward, and fear into determination. Start by asking yourself: What needs to be challenged? What needs to be improved? What is the greatest risk? What can I expect? What can I learn? When we challenge the status quo, we test our skills and we challenge ourselves. The gift of life is to make a difference, and the call of leadership is to say this is not good enough. We have the choice to make things better. When we challenge the status quo, we believe that our abilities will be able to make a difference. What action will you take to challenge the status quo?

My Resilience Journal: Plans and Strategies to Build my Resilience

Chapter Fifteen

Reflect and Rejuvenate

Too much pressure can make a lot of us angry, frustrated, irritable or sad. Over time the pressure and stress can knock you out cold with a burnout. Studies have long shown that stress can have a lasting, negative impact on the brain. Exposure to even a few days of stress compromises the effectiveness of neurons in the hippocampus—an important brain area responsible for reasoning and memory. Weeks of stress cause reversible damage to neuronal dendrites (the small "arms" that brain cells use to communicate with each other), and months of stress can permanently destroy neurons. Stress is a formidable threat to your success—when stress gets out of control, your brain and your performance suffer. How can you deal with pressure and stress before it gets the best of you?

The Trap of Depression

After prolonged periods of relational, work, financial or physical stress, there are very high chances that you can burn out and begin to head towards a major depression. When things become dysfunctional in your life and the people that you expect to support you are sabotaging your progress, it is very easy to get into a meltdown where you find yourself in a state of hopelessness. There comes a time when you don't want to meet new people, carry on conversations, or overload your brain with information. Sometimes you get into a dark frame of mind —clouded by worry, irritation, and self-pity. All you want to do is to get away.

Stop Worrying About What People Think

Most times when we are undergoing extreme pressure in our lives, the people around us may totally have no clue about what is going on within us. You may feel like you want to explode, but you frantically keep kicking your legs under the water. Those around you will be seeing a very calm and collected version of you. Trying to keep these appearances is usually very costly to us and may result in a total breakdown. It is usually the very people who were either causing you stress, putting you under pressure or those you were trying to please that will be the first to ridicule you when you break down. When your sense of pleasure and satisfaction are derived from the opinions of other people, you are no longer the master of your own happiness.

Develop Your Emotional Intelligence to Deal With Toxic People

Whether it's negativity, cruelty, the victim syndrome, or just plain craziness, toxic people drive your brain into a stressed-out state that should be avoided at all costs. Toxic people drive you crazy because their behaviour is so irrational. The ability to manage your emotions and remain calm under pressure has a direct link to your performance. Top performers are skilled at managing their emotions in times of stress in order to remain calm and in control. One of their greatest gifts is the ability to neutralize toxic people. Top performers have well-honed coping strategies that they employ to keep toxic people at bay. To deal with toxic people effectively, you need an approach that enables you, across the board, to control what you can and eliminate what you can't. Successful people know how important it is to live to fight another day. In conflict, unchecked emotion makes you dig your heels in and fight the kind of battle that can leave you severely damaged. When you read and respond to your emotions, you're able to choose your battles wisely and only stand your ground when the time is right. Maintaining an emotional distance requires awareness. You cannot stop someone from pushing your buttons if you don't recognize when it's happening. Sometimes you will find yourself in situations where you'll need to regroup and choose the best way forward.

Reinvent Yourself

In Greek mythology, a phoenix is a long-lived bird that is cyclically regenerated or reborn. Associated with the Sun, a phoenix obtains new life by arising from the ashes of its predecessor. According to some sources, the phoenix dies in a show of flames and combustion, although there are other sources that claim that the legendary bird dies and simply decomposes before being born again. When you've been knocked down, do you know how to get back up again? As human beings, we are all going to feel defeated at some point in our lives. Have you ever experienced your life falling apart all at once? Sometimes life hits us fast and hard and knocks us off our feet for a while. Everyone has times when they endure setbacks, disappointments, and failures.

Motivate Yourself

With so many things that could have come your way thus far in your life, sometimes you find yourself wondering whether your dreams and goals are still worth pursuing after all. Discouragement and distractions can come from so many directions and formats. How do you keep going when the odds are against you? How do you renew your faith to achieve your set goals? What do you tell yourself when there are so many other voices within and around you encouraging you to throw in the towel? How can you grow your mental stamina so that it can fight for you when you don't feel like going on anymore? Goals are meant to be revisited. If you feel so far off path that thinking about your original goal only brings up feelings of guilt and overwhelm, it's time to establish goals and a plan of action that propel you. Sometimes setbacks occur because we need to rethink where we were going, our attitude about a certain area of our life, old thought patterns or beliefs that we've let fester—the list goes on and on. Let this be a stepping stone to greater awareness and don't play into the idea that it's a stumbling block.

Challenging situations can often teach us what we have left to learn. Write in in order to vent your frustrations, brainstorm strategies to get out of it, or write about a more positive time in your life. Read motivational, inspirational, or encouraging words from others. Instead of feeling oppressed by our circumstances, we can use the difficulties we encounter in life to evolve as human beings. When we transform the unpleasant stuff in life into fertilizer for our personal growth, we're able to become wiser. Regardless of what we're going through, we can all develop resilience. It won't prevent the hard times or take away our pain, but it will weave our hurts and losses into the fabric of a richer and more meaningful existence.

How Do You Rejuvenate?

When was the last time you really played hard and laughed? What activities have you invested in that help you to rejuvenate your emotional, physical and mental strength? Do you have a place of escape? Leaving your everyday to find a place of retreat is an important practice in self-care. It helps you to reflect, rejuvenate and add value to your self-concept. If you are going to be able to really love others—to value them, to listen, to respond to their needs effectively—you need to attend to your own needs as well. Take time to restore, renew and rejuvenate yourself so that you can enjoy life a little more and to bring more peace and more happiness into your life. Learn breathing techniques. Take a deep breath and hold it for 5 seconds. Get away. Pamper yourself. Disconnect yourself. Reassess your life. Research various relaxation tips. The best way to rejuvenate yourself is to reduce the amount of stress you have present in your life and rest. When you sleep soundly, your body has the opportunity to repair itself physically and psychologically. A good night's sleep makes you more positive, creative, and proactive in your approach to life. Where you focus your attention determines your emotional state. When you fixate on the problems you're facing, you create and prolong negative emotions and stress. When you focus on actions to better yourself and your circumstances, you create a sense of personal efficacy that produces positive emotions and reduces stress. Self-care often seems like an extravagance. It can seem indulgent, perhaps even selfish but it is very important. Invest in a good support system. Do you need a counsellor, a mentor or a life coach? Identify those individuals in your life and make an effort to seek their insight and assistance when you need it. Something as simple as explaining the situation can lead to a new perspective.

MY RESILIENCE JOURNAL: PLANS AND STRATEGIES TO BUILD MY RESILIENCE

Chapter Sixteen

What Type of Legacy Do You Want to Leave?

When Robin Williams died, Steve Martin called him "a mensch." It's safe to say that everyone considered Robin Williams not only to be a very funny man but also one of the kindest. Calling him a mensch is the greatest eulogy because a mensch is a person who is decent and honourable, a person of high integrity who has genuine care for their fellow mankind. A mensch always looks for an opportunity to do good in life, to be of help to others and to give without regard for anything in return. A mensch does not cut corners in their relationships with people. You always feel safe in the presence of a mensch because you instinctively know that they will not deceive you, undermine you or diminish you in any way. Being called a mensch is the ultimate compliment you can receive. The late Dr Myles Munroe remarked that "the wealthiest places in the world are not gold mines, oil fields, diamond mines or banks. The wealthiest place is the cemetery." What do you want to leave for the world, that will affect it when you are gone? Whether this is for your children, for the community, or for your partner, what effect do you want your living memory to have on people?

Are You Adding Value to the People in Your Life?

We all want to feel more confident. We want to know that we are providing value. We have to find out how to add value to the people in our lives. When we ask the right questions we can add value to those around us. And when we add value to the world, we naturally feel better, we feel confident and we feel fulfilled. Albert Einstein wrote, "Only a life lived for others is worth living." It's actually a paradoxical concept to the way people have been conditioned to think. Many of us have been brought up to think that there is only so much to go around and we must grab what we can before other people get our share. But there is another paradigm which insists on the importance of community, emphasizing our interconnectedness and interdependence. Actually, many of the most important things we can offer others are not limited in supply and, in fact, actually grow by our giving it! When you show love, compassion, encouragement, support and wisdom to others, your supply doesn't shrink. Adding value to others will also bring you opportunity. If you become known as someone who always helps, always tries to find a solution, you'll find that when other people have new projects or exciting things in which they're getting involved, you will be one of the first they would like to include. Invitations will begin arriving completely unsolicited. It's important to add value in an authentic way, in a way that doesn't have an ulterior motive, in a way that is genuine and helpful and unassuming.

Give Your Time by Teaching and Sharing with Others

Knowledge in and of itself is useless unless you actually use that knowledge or pass the knowledge on to others. It is our duty as human beings that if we know something that can help, even just one person, that we release that knowledge into the universe. Sharing your ideas and know-how may be providing a bridge of unimagined of possibilities for one person or be the missing link for a phenomenal breakthrough for another. One way we add value to society is through volunteering to share our knowledge and skills, our labour and our heart.

What Type of Legacy Do You Want to Leave?

Legacy is defined in Merriam-Webster's dictionary as "something transmitted by or received from an ancestor or predecessor from the past." We commonly hear about legacies "living on" today when they continue to affect those in the present. If you go back through time and analyse the most influential legacies, you'll see that they all inspired action through their own action. They didn't just think about doing things, or tell others to do them; they went out and got things done on their own! A legacy isn't only about leaving what you earned but also what you learned, and we all have an opportunity to make a difference. It doesn't call for wealth, fame or even taking giant steps—you don't have to be a Gandhi or a Martin Luther King to leave a positive mark right now, one that will linger long after you're gone. So where can you start? Throughout history, we have been conditioned to look out for ourselves, or no one else will. But if we're consumed with pursuing only our selfish interests, what are we? Leaving a legacy starts with understanding your authentic person identity. What is your purpose and what are your values? How do you want your life to touch others? If you had to do one thing to improve your world, what would your contribution be? How can you increase the well-being of those who depend on you? How can you leave your mark on whatever you do? The answer to these introspective questions will help you develop a meaningful philosophy of life that goes beyond just creating financial wealth. Your words become the building blocks of your legacy. Knowing what's important, what drives you and how you want to be remembered creates tremendous clarity in how you should live your life.

When individuals are clear about their purpose and identity they are ready to enter their relevant earthly assignment and to lead others as well. Every individual who is determined concerning the essence and significance of their lives here on earth and beyond needs to have clarity on these five Personal leadership questions:

Who AM I?
Why AM I here?
Where AM I going?
How will I get there?

What Will Be My LEGACY?

If today was going to be the last day with your partner, family, organisation or community, what would they miss about you when you are gone? What value are you creating today which will be remembered in your legacy when we read your final eulogy at your funeral?

My Resilience Journal: Plans and Strategies to Build my Resilience

ABOUT THE AUTHOR

Cynthia Chirinda is a transformational strategist, peacebuilder, and wholeness coach dedicated to inspiring individuals, families, and communities to heal, grow, and live with purpose. As a minister of the gospel, she integrates biblical wisdom with practical strategies to guide others through life's transitions and into alignment with God's unique calling.

Through her work with Wholeness Incorporated, Cynthia champions initiatives that foster personal development, holistic well-being, and systems transformation. Her passion is expressed through writing, coaching, public speaking, and dialogue facilitation—igniting change, restoring hope, and equipping others to live faith-filled, purpose-driven lives.

Cynthia's published works explore themes of identity, healing, leadership, and wholeness. Her portfolio includes::

- Managing Transitions: Navigating Change with Grace
- You Are Not Damaged Goods series (*Reboot and Start Afresh, Blossom and Flourish, and Transitioning from Tragedies to Triumph*)
- Destination Wholeness: Going Beyond Brokenness
- The Whole You: Vital Keys for Balanced Living
- Can the Whole Woman Please Stand Up!
- The Wealthy Diary of African Wisdom
- The Connection Factor series (for Women, Leaders, and Personal Development)
- Clothed by Love (Fiction)

- Co-authored works: *Success Within Reach, Reinvented,* and *Victorious Anthology*

Her media work includes:
- **Intelligent Conversations with Cynthia**—A platform for transformative dialogue on leadership, healing, and systems change.
- **Women Rising in Africa**—A series highlighting women leaders across the continent.
- **The Extra Mile**—A documentary tribute to women contributing to nation-building and societal transformation.

Cynthia's heartbeat is this: wholeness is not about perfection—it is about courageously embracing each season, becoming rooted in faith, and rising into God-ordained purpose. Her life and work continue to touch lives across the globe with messages of hope, clarity, and restoration.

Connect with Cynthia:
Website: www.cynthiachirinda.com
Email: cynthia@cynthiachirinda.com
LinkedIn: Cynthia Chirinda

www.ingramcontent.com/pod-product-compliance
Lightning Source LLC
Chambersburg PA
CBHW050914160426
43194CB00011B/2400